Still Following the Trail of Breadcrumbs

to Journal Your Way Back Home

Terry Marotta

Ravenscroft Press
Winchester, Massachusetts

We recommend that you read this book *after* you have listened to the CDs; that way, the stories will pour into your ear first, thus taking you by surprise and setting off in your mind all kinds of fireworks, as thoughts and images from your own life begin coming to back to you.

Then the printed pages you hold here can act as an accompaniment, serving as a valuable way to literally *see* how easily and organically the first-person essay or journal entry can unfold.

And yes: we purposely didn't leave room to record things here in these pages. We want you to be writing in your own little notebook or journal, spanking clean or thumbed and smudged. Because the real gift given here is not Terry's to you – you know that already, right? – but rather it is your gift to yourself.

Table of Contents

Part Two (Disc Two):

About the Author

Additional Works

Order Form

Preface

This is a transcript of *Still Following the Trail of Breadcrumbs to Journal Your Way Back Home,* by Terry Marotta, who is talking to you now.

I put this book together with the idea that it would work in two ways: first, as a simple collection of stories for people to enjoy and use to stimulate their own reflections; and second, as a kind of manual or book of instructions for those wishing to form the habit of getting their thoughts down on paper.

The stories come from almost three decades of recording what I see and hear - my job description since the dawn of that long-ago Princess-Diana-dominated Reagan era when women all had poofy hair and shoulder pads as wide as the decks of aircraft carriers. Since 1980, in other words, when I first took on the task of writing a first-person newspaper column, and the job forced me to get out there every day and just plain look around at each unique and irreproducible moment.

But anyone can do what I do. That's my theory anyway, and I aim to prove it to you here.

In each very short chapter of this book I will say some things that look back or ahead or even sideways at our culture and then I will "hand" pen and paper to you and invite you to do the same – that is, sit down and open the taps yourself and see what comes out.

And if the water seems a bit rusty at first, never mind. The more you write the clearer it will become. Keep moving your pen or hammering away at that keyboard and before you know it you will have stopped talking like everyone else and begun talking like your own little self. Maybe if you can really peel back the layers you will rediscover that self who was once 18 months old and happily playing away with language in your crib in those moments before the grownups could come and lift you out and set you down in your busy day.

Busy days are great. On one level we all love a busy day. But in recent years we have grown too busy. In recent years we have forgotten that really what God was hoping was that we might just look around a little and appreciate all the trouble He went to on our behalf.

Recording what you saw or heard or felt helps you do this even if what you are setting down is painful, as it is bound to be from time to time. Pain is OK; crying too. Think how good you feel when you finally unearth an old buried feeling. "So *that's* what's been hurting all along, this little splinter of a memory all dug in and worked under the skin!" But only write about and it starts to loosen; lifts and raises, comes closer and closer to the surface until – look! There it is, right where you can just gently ease it out and the old pain along with it.

So healing is what this book is for too I guess. It's for feeling thankful and for healing and finally for finding someone to tell this stuff to once you unearth it all. What writer said it: that you don't know what you think sometimes until you write it down?

"What was THAT?" Isn't this what you're inwardly saying after something like 98% of what happens to you?

This is your chance to figure out what "that" was. The people you leave behind are going to be so glad when they come upon your nice messy journals with scribbling in the margins, and the doodles you maybe made to get yourself going!

So take the book in the car with you as you drive if you like but be ready, because most of the traffic you encounter will be "inner." It might be better just to sit in your car and listen while you're parked. Or, find a quiet place at home. Or, bring it on your next walk with some headphones.

I will talk for five or so minutes telling my own little stories and then offer you some beginnings for your own entries. If you press 'pause' after each story I'm pretty sure the next thing you will hear will be this new voice. This voice is your own voice, scratchy as it may be at first. Use it. 'Sing,' as the old poets used to say when they talked about writing. You're going to love doing it.

I know I loved making this book, which I did in a sweet little cabin on a dirt road on the shores of central New Hampshire's Big Boy of a lake called Winnipesaukee.

My old friend Roger Baker of Eagle Rock Studios in Albuquerque performed all the sound magic, and brought a lifetime of studio experience to the task, even composing some original music in places to go between the "cuts," or chapters.

The book design gurus of Wendell Center used their keen sense of beauty and proportion to design the cover and lay out the book, based on a crooked and imperfect picture I took looking out my study window one late-August day.

Look at the cover now. That's our ivy trimming the window. That blue china pen holder was my grandmother's, though she never thought of herself as a grandmother. She was just getting used to being a few people's mother when she died at 31 in 1910.

That cut-glass ink stand belonged to her young husband, whom I knew as my grandfather.

And that young woman in the silver frame? That's my big sister Nan the summer she was 35. Witty as Nan is, she has never picked up her own pen, except for the zingy truth-telling letters and emails she has now and then sent up from her home in Florida, so far from our salt-air, freeze-to-death in-winter Boston roots.

This book is dedicated to her, who made all my fun back when we were Nan and Terry Sheehy, and the sun rose every day on the chance for fresh adventure.

Have Fun Decomposing

Sooner or later there are things we all notice in life. We notice for example that our senses don't quite work the way they once did. Me, I can no longer thread a needle without my contact lenses *and* some big old spectacles *and* a magnifying glass to assist me.

We notice that time speeds past. It seems like just last month I was trying to get my bangs to lie down flat so the kids at the dance would think I was cool. It seems like just last week I learned that if you even *think about* turning over to lie on your tummy after the 20th week of pregnancy, a baby can kick you so hard your eyes will cross.

We notice other more poignant things too of course, like the fact that the small season of the lilacs doesn't last at all. We look at them, lovely lavender cones that they are, drooping with the weight of spring and think, "I must gather some to bring inside." We look again and they are gone.

And we notice, ah do we notice - it sometimes take us a while though - that we rush too much in our lives, which is what keeps us from picking those lilacs in the first place.

But if we're paying attention at all there are other things we notice too, like that the lilacs return every year, and always there is that second chance to go back and do better. And if we're lucky we also notice that diminishing physical powers are more than made up for by the less judging disposition. We just plain get nicer as we become more aware of other people's burdens.

Myself I've noticed that life is full of invitations to have fun, every day brimming with the chance for a good laugh.

I think of the day my Sixth Grade boy was waiting for me to finish checking out at our local supermarket. He dropped a quarter into those little vending machines there by the door and fished out a tiny plastic sort of a jigsaw ball which we figured we were evidently supposed to smash into pieces, then try putting back together again.

On the basis of what they chose to call this strange little gizmo, we guessed that its makers were new to English. "The Fabulous Decomposing Ball" it was called and the instructions that came with it, replete with exclamation points, read this way: "(1) Hold in Hand! (2) Drop to Floor! (3) Have Fun Decomposing!"

Well this little haiku had a knot of four or five of us howling there by the cash register, and *for sure* that was something I didn't expect to see happen when I set out that day to follow my same old path to my same old supermarket.

That's the point though; that's just the way most laughter comes: unannounced and as a gift, and as often one given to us by some stranger.

Experiences of this sort have forced me to conclude that that the world just offers up regular helpings of such opportunities for laughter. It just does. And they're ours for the taking...The trick is staying awake enough to notice when you're being offered one.

And what helps me do that is maintaining the habit of jotting down what I see and hear in a week or a day or even just an hour. You can call that keeping a journal but really it's not as formal as all that. You don't have to be someone who writes every day to say you are keeping one. You just have to stay alert and notice what you're noticing. Maybe you don't even have to actually write stuff down, but it sure helps.

This is a book of instructions for staying awake and being on the lookout - for joy, and beauty, and meaning, all excellent antidotes to the blues of every kind. The stories I tell here are true and stem from both the exchanges I myself have had with people and the exchanges I have seen them having with each other. It's a bouquet of little moments that will help you fully inhabit every minute of your waking day.

There's a Robert Frost poem I have always loved in which the poet talks about savoring autumn's beauty as it looked to him on a Northern October day. It goes like this:

> *Begin the hours of this day slow.*
> *Release one leaf at break of day; at noon release another leaf*
> *Retard the sun with gentle mist, enchant the land with amethyst...*

I forget the rest, but I just love that image about enchanting the land. It about summarizes what I offer you here in this little audio book which is the transformative magic that all such enchantments offer.

I mean the chance to *slow down* the all-too-quick progression of our days by savoring them; the chance to see the world not as old and flawed and broken but as shining still, the way we picture it shining, new-made in the gardens of myth and memory.

If nothing else, yours will be a journal about hope even as these stories are about hope and simple joy. Listening to them you will learn again what you already know: how easy and natural it is for us all to live and to wait in hope. How easy and natural it is to look around a little, then say what you saw.

Because we're here now and we won't be here forever. We might as well have fun decomposing, right? And what wise soul said that the journey was the destination anyway?

It is; the journey *is* the destination, all right. And the record you leave of what you saw here is your trail of breadcrumbs, just like the ones scattered by Hansel and Gretel in the woods, which even on the darkest of nights, will help you to find your way home.

The Water Moving Beneath It

Here is just a little more food for thought as we get ready to think about your new hobby as a person who records impressions. Just a little extra boost to help get you into the mindset that will allow you to begin this practice of leaving your own trail of breadcrumbs.

I'm thinking about what went through my head one winter morning not many years ago, when an ice storm made crystal curving sword-blades of the tree boughs and flashed them in the cold light of sunrise.

I had watched from my window as one by one my neighbors emerged from cozy warm kitchens to chip at their automobiles encased entirely in ice, toiling away for 15 or even 20 minutes to crack open just one door.

I dreaded going out there myself. But when an hour later, I did go outside to free my own car, I happened to peer close at that crystal shell that encased it and saw what the sun had quietly done, as a zillion teensy bubbles moved just underneath it; they were beads of water swarming minutely, like some infinitesimal life-form glimpsed under a microscope.

Armed then with a new confidence, I went at the task, which became.... pure *fun* as I pried up the sheets of ice in big jagged panes, and watched them go smash on the frozen ground.

You have moments in your life when there's true joy like that; moments too, when the joy just drains out of things, and, for days you look in the mirror and think "*You* again;" look out the window and think "And you, you imperfect world!"

I started writing my own personal journal the year I was turning ten. I started writing my journal for publication the year I got done turning 30, and I guess I started writing it as much out of the dull ache of the low moments as out of the leaping gladness of the high ones.

I wrote because my feelings came so piercingly. I wrote because I *remembered* so much: I read once in the journal my mother kept all her life an account of the day she baked a special cake shaped like a rabbit when I was very small, which she says in my baby way I dubbed our "eating bunny." A friend of Mom's had come to visit us that chilly March day and brought her little beagle, according to the entry in this yellowing journal of Mom's. I *remember* that woman. I *remember* that beagle. I had just turned three.

I first started to write and market this journal for publication – and by that I mean the weekly column I've been producing for over two decades – because I missed the classroom, where I had spent seven teaching high school English.

I *missed* the way you could make kids laugh, however drowsy or grouchy or pre-occupied they were. Having laughed, they were ready to think; having thought, they were ready to feel, and Lord knows I missed witnessing that. I started to write because I wanted to help people think that way again, or to help them feel and express things themselves, or even just to help them laugh.

All my life I have loved making people laugh. I showed off so much as a kid; made faces, did impressions and used funny voices. My mom had done that all her life too. "Watch out," she'd say to my sister and me "You'll end up with a face like this!" and point to her wrinkles. We didn't care. We thought she was the funniest person ever. She never spanked us or anything though she did once chase us around the dining room table with a hairbrush before dissolving into laughter at the sight of herself.

The year of that ice storm I had been writing a column for 15 years and was the same age my mom had been when she wrote in her journal about that day with the little beagle and the Eating Bunny.

I lived with Mom and my big sister and our grandfather in his house with its widows-walk view of Boston Harbor.

He was our mother's dad and we lived in his big old sailing ship of a house with him because our father went away before I was born - went away and stayed gone - for keeps, as it happens.

Then that kindly white-haired gent died too and the three of us went to live with our pretty and lively Aunt Grace and her husband Uncle Jack - until the day after my middle school graduation when some sad circumstances took him away for good too. Mom tried for a better job to help with the bills and Aunt Grace doubled her pace at earning the Masters Degree that would bring her better pay as a high school Latin teacher. But we still laughed at the kitchen table, same as we'd always done with these two great women around. Nan and I still made faces and snapped towels and kept our spirits up with songs on the radio with the volume turned up high enough so we could just about block out the sound of Aunt Grace, who locked herself in the bathroom certain nights, opened the taps of the bathtub as far as they would go, and sobbed beneath their racket.

I mention all this so you will be reminded of what you doubtless already know: that even sweet and hopeful books like this do not necessarily arise from a life of great good luck and happy tra-la-la but rather from the usual human toll of loss, and luck that is often far from good.

When you take time to reflect and look back at what's happened to you, maybe in a journal or maybe just through quiet reflection, you begin to realize that out of those sorrowful things an extract of joy can be distilled - just as out of the dead petals comes the perfume. Just as out of the crushed grapes comes the wine, alive and sparkling.

As the abandoned child of a single mother, left first by a father she never knew and then by a father surrogate, I thought for the longest time that certain things would never be mine.

Then, one wintry day I went outside to see the world encased in ice as hard as iron against which my efforts could only prove futile - then looked again and noticed the water moving beneath it and in that instant saw it all: That if you take the long view you will see that life wins. That love wins, you might even say. And that all we have ever wanted or needed we can find in one another.

Unknown as the passing stranger may be to me until the moment our paths cross on the sidewalk, yet I am comforted by his smile.

Unknown as I might be to you now, very soon we will no more be strangers. Very soon you will be comforted - delighted too I hope - by the stories and the lessons I have for you here.

By the end of this book you will have scores of beginnings for entries into your own journal, be it a new journal or an ongoing one.

So come then. Walk with me here through these stories. Because together and only together can we banish fear; together and only together can we find the sense of ease and delight that God hoped we might one day develop when, long and long ago, he first set us down, in a Garden.

What Do You Like?

OK let's start with something fun: a little list of your favorite things. What do YOU like best? I read somewhere that asking yourself that now and then is a good first step toward staying cheerful. I gave it a try and I came up with this list:

I like hearing my big sister talk, or tell a story – any story, however brief or telegraphic.

For example: A few years ago now when they still served actual food on airplanes, she flew in from Florida for a short visit and when I picked her up at the airport, I asked the standard questions about how the flight was. "And what did they feed you?" I ended by inquiring.

"A urinal cake for a snack," she shrugged, sketching in her quick shorthand way a pretty fair picture of those dry little "health bars" they often have, "followed by the standard meal: three screws of pasta and an orange tomato."

I've always loved hearing Nan talk.

When my cousins and I were little, she was our first reliable news-source in a world full of grownup evasion. On the more taboo subjects especially, she did her best to give it to us straight: "OK," she told us at the end of one long investigation. "Girls get something called their 'period,' at age 12 or 13. Boys get theirs later - around 18, usually."

She knew just how all the saints died, especially those martyred in really gruesome fashion, and she shared with us the research for her 9th grade term paper on Premature Burial. "If I were a kid today, they'd have me on the shrink's couch SO FAST!" she mused during this last visit. "Hey, by the way," she added, brightening. "I saw this great bumper sticker last week. 'I tried to contain myself, but I escaped!' it said."

So I like that.

Another thing I like is getting up early to watch the sky lighten; to be alone to write in my diary and make a list of all I will do that day.

I also like making this list. "What neat printing!" people often remark, catching a glimpse of it. "Yup," I say. "This way, even if the day itself goes to hell, I can still say 'Well, it was a pretty list.'" They nod; they know how it is.

I like the kind of writing that is so vivid and true you have to keep stopping as you read, to contain your excitement. Eight months ago, someone gave me a novel called *A Mass for the Dead,* in whose first chapter the author describes two little boys, naked and playing, innocently enjoying the years before the "jeweled cross of sexuality" would be laid upon their backs. When I came to that phrase I closed the book, thinking, "This is too great to read in any but the most focused fashion."

I haven't managed to get back to it yet; but I can feel it waiting up ahead for me.

I like knowing something is waiting for me.

A friend remarked last week how sad he sometimes feels when he considers how many of life's highs are behind him now: high school sports and young love; the births of his babies, and the sense of his powers just rising inside him.

I reminded him of those people we haven't met yet, who will love us with loony abandon, past all deserving: I'm talking about our grandchildren, and maybe even our great-grandchildren, who, chances are, will cry harder than anyone else at our funerals.

I like thinking of those we will love later, whose names we don't even know yet.

I like looking to the future in a spirit of hope; resolving to focus always on what remains, and not what is lost.

I like to live in the moment. And this particular moment, I'm feeling so suddenly alert to what is good in my life, I'm either going to call up Nan for some more saucy talk, or dig out that lovely long-abandoned novel.

> • Make a list yourself now, and see where it leads you...
>
> • Write the phrase, "I like..." let's say seven times on your nice blank page with some spaces between each one. Then go back and finish each sentence with whatever comes into your head next. If you run out of steam with that little sentence-stem add the word "when" as in "I like it when... " and then let the sentence go where it wants. Do this five or six times.
>
> • OK, now let's up the ante and write "I just plain love.... (blank) or "I just plain love it when .."

This is a good beginning. Now you begin to at least have a handle on the things and people and circumstances and places that make you happy. Remember and practice them. Revisit this subject often and make whole new lists to add to the old.

Rules to Live By

When I was little, my big sister could get me to do anything. She routinely got me to hurl myself down two flights of stairs by telling me the comforter she had wrapped me in would act as magical padding.

I trusted her is what it was - even years later at Disneyworld when as two women in our 30s we stood waiting to go on what she described as a mind-blowing journey in sight and sound.

Fifty-five minutes we stood in line for that ride, snaking up ramps and past warnings about your sunglasses and your lower-back pain, Nan going on about how the visual effects were just so UNBELIEVABLE, and the asteroids looked so REAL - like they were coming right at you! Strapped into our little car at last, I said, "Just as long as it's not like a roller coaster ride - because they terrify me."

She had time only for a look of shock and apology before we were hurtling through space at 80 mph. Because not only was it a roller coaster ride, it was a roller coaster ride IN THE DARK.

I think of it at the outset of any new enterprise, at the start of any new day because what enterprise and what day *isn't* a roller-coaster ride in the dark when you get right down to it?

So herewith a set of resolutions for the beginning of any new venture. Well. maybe I'd better scale that back and call it a list of my own little rules.

Rule 1: <u>To be More Attentive to Others' Pain</u>
In the heart of Washington D.C. last month, I saw a man 40, frustrated over a fender-bender with a man 70, walk over and push him so hard he fell down in the street. "Call the police!" the old man begged us, for we were in the car closest to him. We didn't have to. Even as he spoke, we saw people, some running to pay phones, some taking out their own cells, some waving to the approaching patrol car. Their willingness to get involved gave me hope.

Rule 2: <u>To Be More Attentive to Other People's Feelings</u>
Once, in a truly misguided moment, I wrote a supposedly funny piece parodying an actual calendar of support groups, and pretending, among other things, that the people involved in the Head Injury Group couldn't remember the time or the date of their meeting. (I still can't believe I did this. I must have been desperate for a topic for that week's column.)

Anyway, my insensitivity so angered one reader that she called the paper where she saw the piece, demanding my column be dropped. Then she wrote a letter for publication so scathing in its description of me and my writing it caused me physical pain to read it. Feeling wounded but still prideful, I sent her a stiff little note of apology.

Then some ten years passed and I got another letter from her, this time complimenting me on a recent column. She signed it with her last name and first initial only.

I wrote back to say thanks of course.

"By the way, I know this is you," I found myself adding impulsively at the end. "And I'm still sorry for what I did."

And she wrote me with an answering mildness. And then we were friends, though we had never met. And I think of her each time I sit down to write humor.

Rule 3: <u>To Stand with Others in Times of Trouble</u>
So often in life there is unexpected woe. In one hard year, two families in our town lost a child and the whole town mourned with them. I myself lost one of my best friends, who once had me for her high school English teacher and thus knew me better than I know myself; and my husband lost his blunt brave New Hampshire-raised Yankee mom. Of those four services, I managed to attend only two and one of the ones I missed was the one for my old student Dorothy, because she was buried quickly and I was out of town at the time and it would have

been very costly to get home in time, which fact leads me with this final rule:

<u>If at all Possible, Get to the Funerals, or Go to the House of Sadness to Express Your Condolences.</u>

Because pretty early on you see it: Life is a roller coaster ride in the dark, all right - and the only magical padding you have comes from the people beside you.

> • Another thing that pads you is your own changing set of resolutions. You might not have too many. I just had four. But open that journal or notebook now and make a list of them.
>
> • Under each rule, say something about how it came to you, mentioning either a way you have observed it or even a way you have violated it at times.

And realize that this list will change too over time so feel free to rewrite it often.

Who Is Around You

Early one cold February morning I walked on sidewalks gritty with road-sand from the winter's many snowstorms.

A man approached, clutching a bag of bread crumbs to his chest. He waded through a flock of pigeons the way a daycare provider might wade through a surging tide of youngsters - cautiously, with small shuffling steps. He stopped suddenly, and in what looked to me like a lovely gesture of surrender, flung both arms up, tossed the bag high in the air and kept on walking.

The pigeons dove as one at the windfall. Sixty birds threw their skirts in the air like Can-Can girls and showed the world their ruffled underpants. The man walked on without a backward glance, talking purposefully to himself now, as if reporting on the drop.

I hurried next to the public library to sit for 30 minutes, and saw a weathered man in his 70s wearing a watch cap. He moved his lips as he read a periodical from the old wooden shelves of this lovely old building. He might really have *been* reading, or he might have been only pretending, the way I was, since really we were both here to get in out of the cold. In any case we nodded gravely to each other when I got up to leave, like a couple of somber prefects proctoring exam-day at Oxford.

It was noon by then but still mighty cold, and so I soon sought refuge in another toasty spot: a coffee shop, whose window-facing tables, raised on a kind of platform, gave its customers a slightly elevated, schoolmaster's view of the sidewalk. From here I could look all I wanted without being looked at, an ideal perch for catching people at their most human.

Across the street, the proprietor of a discount jewelry store talked tirelessly on the telephone. "Discount Jewelry" read a sign on his window. "Highest Prices Paid For Your Unwanted Valuables."

First he stood by the window and talked, then paced round and round the perimeter of his horseshoe-shaped glass display cases. Who was he talking to with this air of earnest pleading, I wondered? His confessor? His bookie? His lady, out of sorts and in need of soothing?

There was no knowing, and my gaze skimmed back toward the pavement - where two young guys wrestled with the forward leg of their pushcart. An illegally parked car prevented them by a fraction of an inch from anchoring it in the cobblestone-rimmed hole just designed for that purpose. One of them, fed up, finally squealed in frustration and gave the car's bumper a good swift kick.

A woman in her 60s walked by then, wearing a baseball cap. With one eye open wide and the other squeezed shut, she had the ironic look of a ventriloquist's dummy winking at the world and all that is in it.

And then? Then a tattered elderly gent trudged past my window and looked up, momentarily stunning me. He could have been any one of my uncles by the look of him, bright-eyed as they were and small-built, and born as this man seemed to have been born not too many years after the last century's beginning.

He must have had a similar reaction seeing me, because he stopped dead in his tracks when our eyes met.

I had to smile at him, he was so familiar. At first he looked away, then looked back fast; then he laid a finger on his chest in the wordless but universal gesture: "Me? You mean me?"

We raised a slow hand in greeting, each maybe remembering someone who looked like the other.

Then he passed and I saw again the jeweler's heart-shaped sign for the Valuable Unwanted. A new feeling flooded my real and beating heart and I knew that for me, that moment and that morning had been Valentine enough. Because really how often is it that someone singles you out with that warm spontaneous no-strings-attached smile?

You can't believe they mean you. "Me?" you almost squeak with grateful delight and all but point to your own chest in the same way as that elderly man had done.

A big part of what I try to communicate in everything I write or say is that we can generally trust each other and really there is no such thing as a stranger.

• What I would like you to try for in this exercise is start something with the phrase "I didn't even know this person and yet here she was" (or "here he was..." and then you can say "...getting down on the floor with me to help look" or "giving me his whole lunch" or whatever. Something will come back.)

• Just try recalling a time when a total stranger acted as a sort of helping angel for you. It won't be hard I bet; it happens all the time!

The Mystical Zap!

Before email came along, letter-writing was beginning to look like a lost art, and what a shame if it became that, for when people write down things, they preserve the moment.

Even decades later, readers can sense the life throbbing beneath their words. As Emily Dickinson said, a letter feels like immortality. She said, "It is the mind alone, without corporeal friend."

Emily herself makes a good example. Though dead these 120 years, she spoke so vividly in the letters written from her yearning and solitary heart that I sometimes think of her as a living friend. She seems just that potent to me. She seems just that familiar.

Like the funny friend you relish hearing from, she possessed a remarkable wit and at the same time a near-saintly brand of perspicacity. "Life is Miracle," she wrote in one letter, "and Death as harmless as a Bee, except to those who run."

As anybody familiar with her poems knows, this thing called Death was something Emily seemed almost to welcome. "Dying is a wild Night and a new Road," she wrote to one friend. And, to another, "There are no Dead, Dear Katie. The grave is but our moan for them."

But elsewhere, she feels as frail and life-torn as any of us. "You send the water over the dam in my brown eyes," she told someone about eyes that were the color of "the Sherry in the Glass that the Guest leaves."

She was addressing a literary bigwig in this letter, to ask if he thought that her verse "lived," meaning was it any good. In the end, he told her it was too unorthodox for the times, but how modest she was, thus baring her timid neck to the critic's sword! "Will you tell me my faults?" she wrote. "Men do not call the surgeon to *commend* the bone, but to set it."

Some found her *too* modest. Fellow writer Helen Hunt Jackson wrote, "You are a great poet, and it is a wrong to the day you live in that you will not sing aloud. When you are what men call dead, you will be sorry you were so stingy."

But if she was modest, she was also passionate, both about writing and about the people that she loved:

"If I read a book and it makes my whole body so cold no fire can warm me, I know *that* is poetry," she writes, talking of her art. And in reference to one of her intimates, "Are you pretty well? Have you been happy? Are your eyes safe?"

When I read these words, I almost *miss* this shy woman, even as I miss the ones who have moved permanently out of my daily own life: my mother, gone these many years to the grave; my sister Nan, moved to faraway Florida.

And yet here they are: In the letters that Mom, a Caroline called Cal, wrote to her sister in the 1950's, wryly signing them "Calcium" or "Calorie" or even "Cow." Or in the jokey emails Nan wrote in the 1990's, describing fictional old folks she calls Aunt Fallopia and Uncle Pendulous.

Emily was right: When I read the words of those I have loved, they are right here beside me.

For me I guess that wild Night on a new Road is not Death so much. For me it is the mystical zap of human communication.

> • Now I want *you* to think back to a letter that just pulled you right up out of your little room and into a different world. Was it summer and you away and the letter coming from home? Was it wartime and you at home and the letter coming from the front?
>
> • Or was it an old envelope you came upon in a box in your very own house, from one now gone forever?
>
> • Try to picture that envelope. Describe the sight of that person's handwriting. Smell the paper in memory to see if you can still bring back the smell of the old stationery, and ink and the dusty bottom of the closet.

Letters travel back and forth along that highway outside of time and space, simply because they hold the passports that allow such travel. If you pick a letter from your past, maybe one that you yourself have written and forgotten about, you can just travel with it. A magic carpet the written word is. You know that. You've always known it....

Oops!

I've been noticing all the ads there are out there for brain-sharpening herbal remedies that play on your worst fears about losing your marbles: "Do you sometimes find yourself *groping for the names of people you know well?*" one says. "Do you *walk into a room and forget why you went there?*" "Do you... *misplace things?*"

Well, but who can't say yes to most of these questions? And as far as groping, forgetting and misplacing go, I've been doing all three since I was young enough to still be watching The Flintstones.

Lately, my own vision having changed to the point where the printing on this sides of the food boxes looked like little dancing insects, I went out and got me some contact lenses - which I keep somehow losing track of when they slide up into that spooky scarlet crawl-space behind my eyes, so I then forget about them, and so put in others, and sometimes others still - until the day comes when my eyes start watering like crazy and dispensing those little disks of plastic, like a vending machine.

But none of this ever bothered me.

It never bothered me that I couldn't recite the Preamble to the Constitution anymore, or even name that book I couldn't stop raving about six months ago (Uh... it was blue, I think.)

It never bothered me that I made mistakes.

Once I was trying to pull something from my oven in a kitchen crowded with family members. I looked and looked for the pair of potholders, finally yelling in exasperation, "Who the heck took the Puff Daddies!" Puff Daddy being the former name of hip-hop king Sean Combs, who has not a thing in common with small heat-resistant squares of cloth. Once I left the tub running on the second floor, causing the light fixture in the kitchen below to spend hours weeping mournful tears. And more than once I have spooned instant coffee onto my cereal, only thinking mildly, "This doesn't seem *quite* right..."

And none of this ever bothered me.

What bothers me is when family members - those same jokers who took the Puff Daddies - just *assume* that I am the author of any bonehead move that gets made around here.

Here's an example:

One wintry night I put in a load of wash and went outside to warm up the car and wait for them all. It was a Sunday and we were just dashing out for a quick bite of dinner. But when they piled into the car, they were all laughing.

"Mum," said the high school junior, "We have bad news." A spate of suppressed laughter followed. My treacherous mate David broke in. "Uh, I heard this... *noise*...in the washing machine just now, so I opened it. There seems to be a ... well a whole box of *cat food* in there with your clothes." And everyone laughed uncontrollably.

So OK, when we got back from dinner, I took a look: and sure enough, thousands of pellets of bloated cat treats were floating lazily around in the brown broth that held my dainty washables.

The worst part wasn't the hour it took to fish them out, one by one. Or the three hours it took to drain the load, skim the pulverized mess and run the whole thing again. The worst part was knowing my family really did think I'd put in cat food instead of powdered detergent - while really the cat food fell off the shelf above and into the washing machine.

I think.

But hey, coffee crystals on your cereal make your mind sharp I tell myself. Anyway I think I read that once in a book called.... Um, called... Well it had this pretty yellow cover.....

You won't need much help with this one!

• Try starting it with "I couldn't believe it myself; what on earth was I *thinking?!*" and then see where it takes you.

• For example, did you ever get all dressed up and go to church – only to realize you had forgotten to put a skirt on over that slip?

• Did you ever mistakenly grab the diaper ointment and start...*brushing your teeth with it?*

• Ever head off for your baby's dedication ceremony with cameras, in-laws, flowers – everything but the baby himself, left sleeping peacefully in his crib?

On Staying Put

Here's another way to make entries in your journal or memory book: begin with one incident and take a couple of great looping stitches back through time to link it to other similar incidents and see what kind of pleasing pattern or themes might emerge. For example what you write might end up like what I say here about the way spring in North America etc...

As most of us know spring in North America will break your heart, the way it grants warmth one day and withholds it the next.

On one of its warmer days, a young woman in her 20s began on her garden. The soil in the tiny yard behind the two-family house where she had begun renting rooms was dank and claylike; but she stepped hopefully onto it, spent the next six hours spreading mountains of loam, and by 5:00 o'clock that day was filthy, sore, and completely happy. I did not see this but heard about the following day.

At twilight on a much cooler April afternoon, a man in his 40s got in some fishing at a little pond. I watched from my parked car as he drove up, then carefully took his gear and his coffee out, setting the coffee down at water's edge and arranging his tackle. Then, for 30 minutes he cast and reeled, cast and reeled, with an air of contentment that was contagious to every jogger stroller and sitter who saw.

§ Before dawn on the morning after a fierce little early-spring snow, a man in his early 60s climbed into his trusty truck now fitted with a blade of snowplow in its teeth and headed out to clear him some driveways. I had driven though this storm the night before, to spend time writing at the summer house we keep on this quiet neck of land that juts into Lake Winnipesaukee. When he reached me along toward noon of this still-snowy day, he took the time to shovel my walk, and seeing my car decided to ring the doorbell.

We visited a bit, and on a whim I asked if I could ride along as he plowed his other driveways.

"Sure," he said. "I've only got but six or eight left."

And so I rode. And I found it thrilling, this going-plowing: the push and pull of it; the rumble and dig; the swooning sense of free-fall as, trusting to traction, you plunge lakeward down the steepest snowy driveways. I loved the artistry of the task and the plain clean physics of it. Like the spreading of plaster, without missing any corners. Like the frosting of cupcakes, without trailing any crumbs.

Under the spell of it, I felt further emboldened and asked my plowing friend in his 60s if he was born here.

He nodded. "Sure, just down the Neck a bit. Then when I was five, we moved about a mile closer to town. Then once I got married I built the house across the road there, where I live now."

I don't know where I got the nerve to ask this next question but it just seemed to flow from this recitation. "And where will you be buried, Joe? Do you ever think about that?"

He hesitated not at all. "Well" he said, "we have a plot in town, but my real dream is to be buried here on the Neck in that old graveyard down 't th' end if I can get leave from the town for it."

I thought a lot about this conversation in the days following that spring storm. About how there are worse things for a man than to live life in one place and to be buried on the same stretch of land where he lay in his bed nights, man and boy alike.

Worse things, and maybe few better.

I thought too of that fellow in his 40s, whom I watched as he fished. It wasn't until he saw me, touched his cap and said "'Lo, Ms. Marotta" that I realized I knew him - from the long-ago time when, several towns away, he had sat as a student before me in the high school where I worked as a young teacher just starting out.

And I thought also of that girl in her 20s digging in her garden, who is my own eldest girl living in that old two-family house with her spouse and new baby; in the very rooms that by fate's circular way are the same rooms in which she had once learned to sit up, and talk, and drink from a cup.

I don't really know I guess how this daughter of mine or that former student really feels about staying so close to home.

But it's pretty clear that the one in his 60s who plowed and the one 50 who rode along after a quick spring snowstorm seemed to agree - that a privilege it is to watch spring advance on familiar hillsides.

> • Now you go back over this day with sharp eyes and just see if you didn't witness a few exchanges or have a few thoughts over the last 24 hours that fastened you snug and tight as an upholstery button into this one fleeting and unique day with one or two or three of your fellow citizens buttoned right in alongside you.

You're are taking big stitches in this exercise, remember; walking on stilts that let you take nice wide strides. Write down one moment that you witnessed, then just see where it leads you.

The Kid with the Popcorn

My sister Nan tells a story about the time in her early 30s when her little girl Gracie brought a friend home and introduced her quickly around, both to Nan's step-daughter, a 16-year-old dressed for work as a waitress in bandbox-fresh clothes; and to Nan herself, the mom of the family, who, decked out in cut-offs and a T-shirt, was just digging, greasy-chinned, into a bowl of popcorn.

It was the outfits that threw the young guest off, I guess, because when she and Gracie stepped outside to swing on the swings she said, "Your mom looked real pretty in her uniform! But who was the kid with the popcorn?"

These days it's harder to tell what role women play or even how old they are by the way they dress and every new season, when the clothing makers try to stuff yet another whole new look down our throats, I am grateful for this fact.

We didn't always have this kind of choice. I didn't have it and I didn't want it. In a desperate lunging effort to gain entrance to the kingdom of glamour, I simply stepped to the music of the marching band called Fashion.

When I woke up to clothes it was to find the whole country's ideal of style influenced by beautiful Jackie, the young President's whispery bride. She had long legs, small hips and wide large eyes to go with the sheaths and pillboxes of the early 1960s.

I was in puberty then, with all its many torments, and had hips distinctly unsmall and the albatross of a violin case that bumped against people's legs on the bus. In fact I had the Wrong Look even before you even got to the clothes with my crazy black curls and a forehead so high you could show movies on it. In my mind I looked like Clarabell on the old Howdy Doody Show, with my hair the biggest problem. In an effort to improve it, I ironed it, and of course slept nights on metal rollers with tiny metal spikes driven into my skull like cloves in a Yuletide orange.

The night of the Sophomore Social, my sister Nan with her own hair in soft honey-colored wings framing her china-doll face, offered to do my hair for me. First she teased and sprayed it into a wide sticky cloud, then tried collecting it into a French twist. It resisted. With all the teasing it had grown in volume, like a fungus, risen like a yeast.

And then there were those unconquerable curls, which, having begun to multiplying like busy third-graders, were now coiling in corkscrews about her mightily striving fingers.

Thirty minutes in, she put down the brush. "I can't do this," she said, and walked away. My date came and I greeted him looking like the Bride of Frankenstein. He danced all night with the punchbowl, I with my old pal Disappointment.

Mercifully for us all, it wasn't long after this that vast tectonic plates of change began shifting beneath the landscape of American society. The Beatles had come. The Mamas and the Papas too, who pretty much went around in their pajamas anyway. Mini skirts happened and Woodstock and big floppy hats and suddenly you wore what you felt like wearing.

And this spirit of diversity has persisted, it seems to me, and has maybe even extended from how people dress to how they live their lives. We could all feel good about this if it were so, especially the parents of kids just taking on the formidable adversary of peer opinion.

A decade or so ago, when minis again came back in a big way, Gloria Steinem was spotted in one. What was she thinking, the press wanted to know, a feminist like herself knuckling under to the dictates of fashion? But she had a good answer for them I thought: She said it wasn't so much a question of fashion these days as it was a question of style. Folks feel free to find their own style today, she was implying, wear clothes they find both comfortable and expressive to the world of who they are.

I know I go about dressed more spontaneously now than I used to in the old lock-step days of my fashion-conscious youth. And like Nan with her face chin-deep in her popcorn, I may look a little incongruous at times. But it's how a person feels inside that counts, I guess. And me? I feel free and comfortable and fine.

• So now let's see what comes back for you. Try starting a sentence like this:

• "It was the night of the big dance and I *still* wasn't sure about what I was wearing." This would be a good first sentence because you can tell about an outfit; just lay it all out on the bed for us, whether you're a man or a woman. People are natural voyeurs; everyone loves descriptions of people getting dressed and what you wore to your high school dance will evoke a whole era for you.

• Close your eyes now and try seeing all the different parts, like the accessories and the undergarments, like the buttons and the cummerbunds.

> • "It was the night of the big dance" (or if you prefer) "it was my wedding day" "and I only had 20 minutes to dress and be ready."

Try that beginning if you think it might work better you.

Fannytime

At the start of each new season I think about ways to improve myself; design a little "unit" to try and learn new things, just like the schoolkids do.

Last fall, for example, I listened to a whole set of vocabulary-building tapes, which taught me nothing so much as how drenched the English language is in Latin derivatives. And hearing all that Latin again brought me to the memory of the way my girl Annie won an actual cash prize at her college commencement for learning Latin so well. She used to go to this pub in town and work away with her Latin dictionary on all those mystifyingly dense passages, while a crowd of geezers would tease her for spending so much time on a so-called dead language.

"No money in Latin, Annie!" they would taunt. "Never make any money in Latin you won't!"

Ah, but Annie knew that to learn a thing really, you had to put in a certain kind of time. In some quarters that time as known as Fannytime.

In Fannytime, you simply sit with your subject, trying to understand it. Not jumping up for drinks of water or scribbling-sessions in your date book. Not even worrying if you'll ever "get" it. When writer Annie Dillard works on a manuscript she says she sits up with those imperfect sentences the way a person sits up with an ailing friend.

Anyone who seeks to gain mastery over a body of knowledge needs to do this. To learn certain poems, or the elements on the Periodic Table, or even just the list of English prepositions, you *have* to do this. You have to put in Fannytime.

And you'll be glad that you did, because it sure-enough works.

I wasn't great at U.S. History. All those dates made my head spin. But my 11th grade history teacher promised he'd take out to dinner the kid who got the highest grade in the History SATII (then called the History Achievement.)

This boy named Sam Poulton was the favorite student of our History teacher Mr. Trull; anyway, Mr. Trull was always calling on him. And I couldn't stand thinking of the two of *them* going out, little male club that they were.

So, a month before the test, I bought three giant pieces of poster board, sat down at the dining room table where I'd done all my homework from Grade Six on, and copied every review term out of the back of each chapter, along with definitions and salient facts.

It took me days. Nights. Whole weekends. In a month's time I had copied them all down in the teensiest writing; just copied them, and the night before the test, re-read them all through, hoping that would suffice.

It did. I didn't beat Sam Poulton, but I scored higher in U.S. History than I did in any other SAT; in History, my second-lowest subject! And even now, if you're looking for the definition of Manifest Destiny, I've got it for ya. The meaning of the Dred Scott Decision? Got that too. Marbury vs. Madison? 54°40' or Fight? The Zimmerman Note? Got 'em all, baby, etched on the little hard-drive of my central cortex.

And as with bodies of knowledge, so with human beings: If you want to understand them, quit talking and sit down with them. Let THEM talk. You listen and be glad for the privilege.

You might ask what Annie did with that prize money she won on her last day as a college senior, and did she by chance stop in at that tavern and buy a round for the nice mocking geezers who kept her company with all those thorny Latin passages?

She sure did, though she teased them a little bit first, saying, "No money in Latin eh?" She was a good girl all year long, sitting down every day with that knuckly dense old language with its verbs all at the end of every sentence. She couldn't have mastered it otherwise. But the guys on the bar stools up front might have been the ones who really made the difference. Because we can't do anything alone; we really can't.

• Think back to an enterprise you really focused on and maybe surprised even yourself by mastering in the end.

• Was there anyone in the background helping you keep your spirits up, joshing you maybe with their own version of 'No money in Latin, Annie'? Who was the person or who were the people that kept you at it just by sticking around? You might have to reach back in time for this one but that will be fun. Remember we were all pupils? (What a great word, "pupils"!)

Ok pupils, here comes Recess. I just gave you the ball. Now stand up, then stretch a little and come back and kick it around some.

School, I Once Thought...

Things just feel a little different when school starts drawing to a close.

Even we grownups sense it, we for whom the late bell is but a memory. A memory too the collecting-up of textbooks after the year-long loan; the calling in of library volumes, with their endearing grade-school titles: *Our Friend the Panda. Your Solar System. Young Teddy Roosevelt, Rough Rider of Destiny...*

There is, at the school-year's end, that delicious sense of closure. William Butler Yeats was asked once how he knew he was through tinkering with a poem and it was really finished. "It clicks shut," is what he said. There is the same sense of finality about so many end-of-the-school-year rituals; a sense of the thing well and truly done, the case closed, the blackboard finally erased.

I went to two college commencements within the space of one weekend and came away marveling at both all that has changed in this old rite of passage, and all that has remained the same.

At the first one, the academic gowns the kids wore were made from goods of such cheesiness as to resemble that maddening kind of plastic wrap that doesn't so much cling to as hover about the food it seeks to cover. They didn't hang right. Their seams puckered. Their hems dipped and rose. And, in the breezy way of the times, many kids didn't even bother zipping them. Several young men marched with tee shirts and boxers under their gowns. One young woman wore a dress, and her academic gown over the dress, and then a long ratty sweater over the gown.

A young friend attending this ceremony with me had recently endured a commencement of his own.

"You should have been at *my* graduation if you think this is informal," he whispered as these other young graduates passed.

"They gave me a robe so short it looked like a dickey, and when the time came to actually hand us our diplomas, they just had us line up in a field, where a sort of lunch lady pulled them one by one from a file cabinet."

Two days later, at the second college commencement, the gowns at least fit better, though these kids "customized" their outfits too, with feather boas, and fanciful armbands, and whimsical headgear in place of the traditional academic cap.

And the parents in this audience seemed to express themselves with a similar whimsy: A family from China stood and hooted when their daughter's name was read. A family from Kenya did the same when their turn came.

And a family from Brooklyn who sat in front of us outdid them all. When our own graduate's name was read, and we too exulted in our more staid New England way, the Brooklynites wheeled around. "Ya shoulda told us!" they boomed amiably. "We'da helped ya yell!"

This ceremony was over three hours long. For over three sweltering hours we all sat, alternately re-reading our sweat-soaked programs and fanning ourselves with them. I studied the name of every graduate, departing trustee, and distinguished professor. Then I dug out the program from the Baccalaureate Service the day before and studied that.

In that service, the soon-to-be-graduates recited a lovely responsive prayer together with the college president.

"We seek to understand the shyness behind arrogance, the fear behind pride, the anguish behind cruelty," she had read.

"All life flows into a common life, if we will but open our eyes to our companions," the young people had responded in unison.

Reading these words cooled and softened me then, to the point where I stopped my ceaseless evaluations and thought only this:

It doesn't matter where you stand or how you dress getting your diploma; whether you get it from a dignitary robed like the Pope or a seeming lunch lady elbow-deep in file folders. The point is you made the grade. Your school days are behind you. And nothing you ever do will be as easy again.

> • Now let's try writing something that begins: "I once thought school was a place where .... but really ..." and you fill it in and take it from there.
>
> • Or "I used to see school as being....but now I realize it was more like ..." and see if that takes you somewhere nice.
>
> • Or you could write down "I went to college thinking I would learn..." etc. "but instead I found out..." More to say? More there?
>
> Any one of these ought to be fruitful for you. Or you can make up your own beginning. Take plenty of time and don't worry about the bell; they've extended the period for us.

Take a Sad Song
and Make It Better

I am a white lady who, together with her white spouse, has helped bring several young black men toward adulthood. I met these young men because my town maintains one of the residential public school chapters of the National Program for a Better Chance, which identifies talented minority youth in educationally disadvantaged communities and brings them to over 200 fine public and private secondary schools around the country.

I am also an old high school English teacher who left the classroom to raise her babies. After five years swimming in the rich tidal pool of parenthood, I still missed adolescents so much I was thrilled, when we moved to our new town, to be invited to volunteer with its ABC program, which every year raises all revenues necessary to feed, house and otherwise support the seven or eight young men going to high school here. Over time, I served as Writing Tutor, Enrichment Person and eventually Host-Mom to one of them.

Although that first host-son ended up leaving the program early, he never left our lives or lost touch with his two best pals still in it. And even after all three finished high school, all three stayed close, coming back to live with us, sometimes for months or even a year, as they made their way though college. Today one has two boys himself. Another lives in New York to be near his ailing mom. The third, our original host son, is the acknowledged eldest brother in this family, who over the last ten years has put a shine on every Christmas morning, birthday dinner, and weekend ballgame.

But a white lady with three black sons sees much she did not see before. Once, on a road trip when the guys were 14, we stopped for snacks and they tumbled from the car in high spirits. Five minutes later they were back, their faces drained of blood. "What happened?" I asked at once.

"Nothing," said one immediately.

"Somebody called us niggers," said the other.

This white lady learned a lot through their young pain; learned even more a decade later when one of them, then 25, after doing his weekly banking in this same good town of ours with its fine and caring people, stopped to use a pay phone.

He came here directly afterward to tell about it. "A cop approached me just as I was dialing," Chris said.

"*Can I help you?* he said in a nasty way."

"Oh, Chris," I said. "Did you tell him who you *were?*" Meaning, I suppose, a son of this town, a state champ in wrestling, and one who had brought glory to its name?

"I told him nothing," replied Chris tersely. "'Obviously, I'm making a phone call,' I said. Terry, it's just not worth it."

I feel sad to be reliving these scenes here. But suddenly I am recalling a third scene too, that took place the early-September night before I returned a fourth honorary son of ours to Brown University where he would begin his senior year.

Horace is a young man of color too. He and I had grown close since meeting in his 12th grade year as an ABC scholar and we'd made a ritual over the last four years of going out to dinner together the night before we packed my van to the roof with his stuff and brought him back to school. He and I both have always enjoyed the kind of looking-back and looking-ahead that people do at such junctures anyway and Horace was doing some of that this night.

He got a little worked up when our conversation turned to the topic of hypocrisy, that virus of adulthood that all young people sooner or later come to see as everywhere prevalent; he talked for quite a while about it and with some passion.

"The world is so... FLAWED!" he finally concluded, shaking his head sadly and looking down at the dinner he'd scarcely touched; then he looked up and added with his beautiful smile, "So what can you do but love it?"

I find myself so moved every time I remember this utterance of his.

> What I would like now is for you to try writing something about this flawed world and its effect on you. Try to think of a time when you wanted to give up on it entirely until some little miracle of perception occurred that caused you to turn around and embrace it again.
>
> • But how would you start such a piece? How about by saying, "I was done with them all; in my book that day people were a bad bunch and I was ready to wall off my heart from them for keeps." And keep telling until you come to the point where you soften.
>
> • Then ask yourself, what makes *you* soften? Who or what brings you back into the game? Who or what makes *you* say "the world is so flawed. So what can you do but love it?"

Parts of these exercises won't be easy to complete of course but that doesn't mean it won't still be good for you to try to do them. What do they say about the areas of great pain in our lives and how we can best come to terms with them? "The only way out is through"? Try believing that as you go back and look into those dark caves where bitterness still reigns. Remember that you can't let go of such feelings without bringing them into the light first.

What We're Responsible For

Has it ever been easy to get a child out the door in time? As little kids, they go completely limp when you try to dress them. You feel like an undertaker trying to put pantyhose on a dead person. I think of the times I had to lug my kids like armfuls of cordwood into the play ground of the pre-school. That's another gift they have: When they feel like it, they can increase their molecular density, like Superman, so you can't pick them up. Then too when they feel like it they can turn their legs to rigatoni so you can't set them down.

And as for getting them there on the early side, forget about it.

We remember more than we first realize about our childhoods. Turns out I remember being put to bed while the sun still shone, and taking liquid vitamins through a little dropper, and being zipped to the neck into a medieval sleepgarment designed to prevent me from sucking my thumb.

My sister and I attended this school that was a weird throwback of an old place, with uniforms of a heavy wool serge, like the Union Army wore. These came with a stiff collar-and-cuff set that had to be washed, starched and ironed every time you got a little grape jelly worked into the fibers. It made our mom all the more frantic, having to drop back a century just to get us dressed every day.

And so mostly what I remember about those years is careening toward school in our old station wagon each morning, Mom wild-eyed at the wheel. All the yelling! All the suspense that went into getting the three of us into that car!

I was thrilled when we moved to a new town and I could start taking the bus. I dawdled some, and got Detention some for being late. I didn't mind. You could get a good head start on homework in Detention. And anyway, I figured the tardiness issue was *my* business, and getting to school on time was *my* responsibility, to honor or not as I saw fit from day to day.

Trouble is, I still felt that way as a parent: as if I alone were the one responsible for my children's punctuality - even though I knew they should be held accountable pretty early on for it.

What wars we waged over morning lateness! What battles we fought over whose fault it was! I would say it was their fault. (They'd fuss with their hair; they'd misplace their homework; they'd try leaving the house in blizzards without their jackets on.) And they would say it was mine. (I'd keep stacking the dishes; I'd start folding the laundry.) Either way, when you're the one expected to provide the Ride it's one tension-filled trip to the school house.

The best thing that could have happened to us happened when our kids one by one turned 15 and began attending a different school, each one in turn taking three kinds of public transportation to get there and back.

In the very first week of our oldest girl's year at this school, she missed the last rush-hour train home and called from the station to say she would be taking a later one.

"Should I come get you?" I blurted out, feeling instantly responsible.

"Oh No," Carrie said. "But this... *man* keeps introducing himself to me. He's very sweet and you know maybe a little retarded. Anyway we've shaken hands three times already; then, for a while, he was resting his head on my shoulder–"

"Why don't I come in and get you!" I interrupted, slapping my pockets as I felt for my car keys.

"No, really!" she said mildly. "I'm fine!"

And you know what? She really was fine. She was responsible about awaiting the next train and she handled herself perfectly in the company of her benign friend, who in any case soon enough fell into a peaceful slumber a few yards away. Maybe it turns out that the sooner your kids learn about life's quirky rhythms, the sooner they can fall in step themselves.

It also turns out that all kinds of people can wait with us and help us on our way. Carrie's companion at the train station found solace in her company, and I still believe it might have been something in his sweetly trusting way that made her from that day forward into the kind of person who *never* hurries past when spoken to; who *always* stops and acknowledges the humanity of the one speaking to her.

• So now let's see what you can come up with in the category of the chance stranger who you stood by for a while.

• Or if that yields up nothing listen to this track again to help uncover images from your own early childhood. Maybe some of your own late-for-school stories?

• Maybe the chaos factor as you recall it on schooldays of your own, as either parent or youngster?

You're beginning to see I hope that it doesn't matter *what* your jumping off place is, because the river you jump into is your life.... I'll be quiet now and let you use this lens that is your memory to peer down and down through those still clear waters for what awaits you in their quiet depths.

Amethyst

Sometimes if you look inside and find nothing to write about it's a good idea to look *outside.* The world, and nature in particular, will never fail to serve you up something so arresting you'll be reaching for your pencil before you know it.

I have had feelings on certain autumn days that I've never forgotten. For example, October always moves me with its skies as blue as turquoise, its trees the colors of chrysanthemums, pinned like fat corsages to hills and gardens.

But then November comes and the corsages all fade. Bright tones of burnished bronze and fiery copper mute to hues of taupe and umber. Even the sky itself seems changed in November, its eye-hurting blue more veined with white somehow. It looks moister to us, streaked with what we know will be the clouds of winter, snow-seeded and gathering; gathering.

October is all parade music: The Tuba's big loud oomph. The rattle of snare drums. Great big brass instruments brassily played.

November by contrast is chamber music, played in a minor key. It is string and reed instrument, rather than brass and percussion. It is the oboe's measured sob, the sustained and tremulous sigh of violins. In its small span of days, it is a season unto itself. And in this month you see Earth as she really is, undressed of flounce and ruffle.

Close your eyes and let it be November now in your mind's eye. Walk outdoors and subtract the leaves and flowers, the heavy hanging globes of fruit and vegetable, for they are gone. And yet there is beauty all around you, the good bones beneath the skin: earth's architecture, in all its grace and proportion.

The wind picks up, come November. It scours and polishes; works a practiced hand in the corners of all creation; lifts the sweepings of gardens and makes them spin in dizzy circles.

Then things feel tidied; and animated with a freshened vigor. The squirrels feel it. They draw quick furry arcs as they frisk and caper. The children surely feel it. Sensitive creatures that they are, they sniff the wind to sense which way it is blowing.

Two six-year-olds rang my doorbell one November day and asked to rake our leaves, purely for the fun that was in it. They did rake them, in mounds too wide and scattered to possibly pick up; rang the bell again and pronounced the job done. Gravely, we gave them each a dollar.

Later that day I drove in my car and saw a line of third-graders assembled by a forest for what was clearly a field trip. A small nametag-wearing contingent of parents lingered at the edges, stiff with cold, mittened hands thrust deep in their pockets.

The kids themselves didn't notice the chill. Lined up by twos, they jostled and hip-checked as the teacher explained in a loud outdoor voice. At last they started moving into the woods. "We're walking!" she shouted after them, but she spoke only for herself. The rest of them were jumping, hopping, dancing; I didn't spot a single walker ...

Then toward around 4pm I went to a town pond and saw an old man sleeping in his car, his mouth open like a baby bird's. Near him, on an oak bench, a bundled person in a knit cap winged bread crusts at some ducks. A lone goose bobbed like a cork on the water, whose surface brisk winds had lifted into cowlicks.

I knew that at some point soon this pond would be frozen. I realized that the deep indigo of early evening was just settling on commuters waiting at bus stops. I envisioned many deliverymen hurriedly stitching together shops and houses in their rounds in and out of buildings.

I knew that an hour on, most would be home, lighting lamps by sofas and beds; knew too that a month on, holiday lights would festoon these streets and roadways; knew that two months on, the snow would have spread her linen cloth on every bush and hillside.

But this day was still an autumn day, with a morning that flashed like amethyst or topaz, with a noontime that glowed soft as the milky opal; and setting down a few descriptions of it helped me both to relish it and inhabit it fully.

• Now you try writing about the season you're in right now.

• You'll need to go outside and feel the air on your face. It's fine to sit in your car because you're protected in it. Go someplace in your car where no one will question you, some park or playground or pondside place, a place where there are other people in cars just looking out at the day. Their looking out will help you direct your gaze out.

• Stretch your legs and settle in. Turn off the radio and listen to the wind.

• Notice any birds that come by and watch how they interact with the people.

• Watch the people and see how this day affects them. They are here to see it too. To really *see* any one day is to feel grateful for it and so to journal is to offer prayers of thanksgiving in a way.

Fun with the Language

You can have a lot of fun with a language if you're new to it. Somehow you're not held as much to words' usual meanings.

Little kids have all kinds of fun with language, not just because they're so new to it but because they call things as they see them. When my girl Annie was little, she had both a doll name Scribble-Head (because someone had once scribbled all over its bulbous plastic noggin) and a stuffed doggy called Tunafish (because that's what he came to look like after one trip too many through the Spin Cycle.)

Then too, kids also don't always *hear* a word right, with often amusing results: At age four, one of my nieces used to sing loudly of that mischievous Someone in the kitchen with Dinah, "strummin' on the old man's Joe" as she had it - a potentially painful sort of practice whose jolly rendering in song didn't cause this child to so much as bat an eye.

Word maven and longtime author Richard Lederer has amassed an amazing record of the mistakes kids make with the language at every stage, as they make their way through the curriculum. Achilles' mother dipped him in the "River Stynx" one kid wrote in dead earnest, thus causing him to become "intolerable." Socrates died from an overdose of "wedlock," penned another.

Of course sometimes kids *enjoy* getting the words wrong, not just for the bracing kind of fun they sense they can have with them, but because they know it bothers the heck out of grownups.

A friend suggested once I check out my local paper's Club Calendar section for the weird names young people give to rock bands and sure enough: here were "Mixed Nuts" and "Glazed Baby," "Slughog" and "Dog Bowl." The trick seems to be to arrange the words in ways that are just this side of familiar and yet their effect is unexpected. "Hank of Hair" would be a typical name for a rock band, I guess, or possibly "The Dismembered," to *really* make the old folks gag.

But probably nobody makes such a wild stab at language as those folks most newly arrived on our shores.

I went to a Thai restaurant recently, where the effort to named dishes either with an exotic Oriental mysticism or else a jaunty American zip yielded a truly epic bill of fare.

It took scanning the whole menu to realize that certain odd-sounding dishes had one thing in common: "Buddha Delight", "Queen Smile" and "King Body" weren't just dishes commemorating gods and royal family, and when I came to "Three

Company," I realized: they also showed that their author had not yet learned about apostrophes.

It looked as though that author *did* know about cannibalism, to judge by his word choice, and even seemed to actually encourage it – because here was a dish called "Hearty Sweethearts" and another dubbed "Spicy Friend." But if you preferred to eat animals rather than people with whom you've had a relationship, you could chow down on "Excited Chicken" (doubtless more toothsome than the sedated kind) or "'Dancing Duck" (meaning I guess a duck too excited to just sit there.)

The menu's author offered the cheerleading favorite "Pacific All the Way" and the mysterious "Underwater Dream," as well as that real surprise package," Sea of the Sea." Even the coyly described "Green Awesome with Black Fungus" recalled the rhythms of American slang. It wouldn't have surprised me to read about entrées dubbed "Yo Roaches!," "Man Alive!" or "How's It Goin'?"

Still, you have to give people credit for the valiant attempt to master language, which is one of the chief things that truly separate us from the animals. The chickens may dance, the ducks may get excited; but what's the good, if they can't talk about it?

• OK maybe it seems mean to dredge up lists of phrases people got wrong, but they sure can be funny. How could we help laughing when we discovered one of our own children gravely reciting the Lord's Prayer when small? "Our Father, a rotten Heaven" she began and moved on in the same vein clear through "Thy kingdom come I will be dumb..." And who wouldn't laugh on learning about the Beatles fan who loved Lucy in the Sky with Diamonds, really wailing happily along when she got to the part where the "girl with colitis goes by"?

• So now see what comes up when *you* remember back to phrases you or yours got wrong. Failing that, go to an exotic restaurant whose owners are still new to the language and read the menu like I did. Or sometimes even just the name of the restaurant will make you smile. I saw one in Spain a few summers ago whose whole front was bedecked with the good old Stars and Stripes. "American Restaurant," it read. "Thanks God Is Holiday!" A little wrong yes but sweet too, isn't it?

Who Else Could I Be?

Sometimes come Halloween time I ask myself: Who would I dress up as if right now today they announced an actual Halloween for grownups?

Back in the old days, little girls went out dressed as princesses or kitty-cats on Halloween; as witches or ghosts, if they could stretch far enough toward the dark side.

Little boys seemed to resist the whole dress-up thing somehow, maybe because they got stuffed into jackets and ties a lot more back then. Maybe it felt to them like yet another conspiracy on the part of the females in their lives to deck them out like fools - then go taking their pictures even.

I guess the boys went out dressed as hobos, most of them, borrowing outsized castoffs from a handy male grownup, smearing their faces with charcoal.

My older sister Nan and I went out as hobos ourselves, come to think of it.

Nan set the whole tone for my whole childhood with her nose for the slightly.... 'transgressive' as the saying goes. For one particularly instructive period during a certain autumn, a dead cat came to our attention in an alley we then began visiting the way pilgrims visit a shrine.

("A corpse!" we exulted on first discovering it, giddy with that blended jolt of joy and revulsion. We'd have gone out that Halloween CARRYING the dead cat if we'd dared to. If we hadn't by then taken the common childhood pledge to shelter our grownups, innocents that they were, from life's spicier side.)

Today of course males of every age are far more "plumed" than they once were, and less fixed on the need to seem macho too. It's my sense that these days little boys' costumes are as elaborate as little girls.' This year they will be once again going out dressed to the nines, maybe in masks portraying horror-movie villains: Jason. Chucky. Sometimes even old Tricky-Dick Nixon, who still enjoys a strange afterlife in the Rogue's Gallery of your standard costume shop.

And the point will be what it's always been: To startle. To counter expectation.

We had a good friend back in the 80's. Didn't smoke. Didn't drink. Took old bikes from the dump, fixed them up good as new and gave them to kids who didn't have bikes. On the Halloween immediately following one lunatic's murder of several people by slipping poison into random Tylenol bottles, our friend took his kids around for Trick or Treat, himself dressed as a giant Tylenol capsule - and was actually surprised when another dad offered to punch his lights out. THAT escapade countered all our expectations.

By partying indoors on Halloween, you can cut down on offers of violence (depending on who you friends are of course) and have fun too - by seeing the dedicated beer guzzler show up dressed as a Mormon elder, say, or the biggest Don Juan in the group come decked out as the Pope.

I don't go in for much in the way of girlie stuff; never even wore makeup til I got to be 50. But one year at an adult Halloween party I dressed as Early Cher, in heavy mascara and spangly bathing suit top and hip huggers, and of course a giant wig exploding in cascades of inky curls.

I looked plain ridiculous. It was awesome. And my mate, as Sonny to my Cher, looked even better, in the 70's-era peasant shirt our kids found for him, and some baggy bohemian pants and a Prince Valiant-style wig. Of course with his wire-rimmed glasses, he looked more like early John Denver, or actually with the wig more like Moe of the Three Stooges than either of those two, but still - he SEEMED like Sonny Bono.

That's the fun of Halloween: getting to *seem* like someone else for the night.

• So pick up your pen now and write down who you would "dress up as" if the party started in just 12 hours.

• Or write about the best fun you ever had dressing up. See where that leads.

• If you're feeling especially expansive right now sit down and let your pen tell you who you might you have been if you hadn't chosen this path. Let the image of that old Halloween costume guide you and just remember back – to when you were Silly Putty, warm in the hand and nothing at all had been pressed into you yet. Hmmmm. An astronaut? A ballerina? Lots of little boys want careers where they get to drive a dump truck or a front-end loader. What comes to mind?

The Wicked Elsewhere

Here's a topic we can all identify with: the birds and the bees!

Once, grownups thought it was harmful to say much to kids about sex, or even the body.

My sister Nan and I had a mother who shut the door right in our faces to change her clothes - sometimes just to pull a pair of shorts on under a skirt. As a result, we didn't know what women's bodies looked like until we were old enough to begin coming upon statues of half-naked ladies. As for how males looked, fatherless and brotherless, we had no clue, and even hanging around public statuary didn't help. All the marble guys *we* ever saw had fancy little oak leaves growing out of their groins, which left us *really* mystified.

We stayed mystified, too - right on through childhood.

Then, with a world-weary sigh, our pal Jimmy Rutstein gave us the real lowdown: "When you get married, right after the wedding they take you in a back room where they tie you together by your underpants."

Stunned, we pictured our parents joined like Siamese twins, one even walking upside down maybe. It *couldn't* be true! And yet some part of felt true.

So, what then? Did grownups only *pretend* to live in our sunny world of countertops and kitchen tiles while truly inhabiting some wicked Elsewhere, filled with the strange and unconveyable? And why, come to think of it, did they go silent at so many of our questions? When I saw a dispenser for what we now call "feminine products" in the older girls' bathroom one PTA night and said, "Look, Mom, napkins we can buy and take to the Cafeteria!" why did she just keep walking? When it said right on the machine how sanitary they were?

Lucky for us, Nan got hold of a pamphlet called "Growing Up and Liking It," that showed a tomboy in ankle socks peering in the mirror to see reflected there a prom-ready version of herself, hair swept up in a bun, athlete's body swaddled like a larval moth in 20 yards of gauzy fabric.

We lived, back then, in a big shadowy house complete with secret stairways and a benign circling pantheon of old folks. Far from these elderly saints and far from Mom, we holed up and started reading. We learned about the lunar cycle and studied the hieroglyph of the female reproductive system.

We learned about periods, in other words.

But what was sex then? That impulse, secret and sudden, whose bass note even *we* could hear, humming deep in earth's center?

It was something private, for sure - and more than vaguely forbidden.

Our sexual selves, our fleshly selves: somehow we couldn't get a perspective on either one. Not in the steamy cars of our high school boyfriends and not in our college dorm rooms, in the delicate negotiations involved when a date slept over. The intimate moments most of us had often felt furtive, and swooned into. As if they *befell* us somehow, and we didn't choose them. As if they took place in a world bearing no relation to the daylight world of sports and lunch and homework.

It was two worlds then, and the bridge between them was down. You talked to your date, or else you closed you eyes and journeyed to Planet Elsewhere.

I married mere moments after graduation, I think at least partially to bring those worlds together. And ten years later, I had a nascent writing career, a washing machine and a chorus of wee children who wept like the newly bereaved if you didn't let them come into the bathroom with you and unwrap all the tampons.

The world was changing.

A woman 70 leaned toward me at a Smith Club event we were both at – I'm a proud graduate of that awesome women's college. "My daughter gave me a copy of *Our Bodies Ourselves*," she trilled.

"It recommends buying certain little gadgets and doing your *own* pelvic exams!" It seemed fine with her. I thought sadly of my own mom, unable to explain Kotex to an eight-year-old.

It seems talking about the body isn't half as harmful as NOT talking about it; for the body is valiant and serves us well - even as it allows us to serve and tend each other. And sex, it turns out, takes place not in the Wicked Elsewhere but in the Holy Here. It ties us together, all right - by our spirits, if not by our underpants.

• So now you take a minute and dream back to the earliest rumors you ever heard about Planet Elsewhere. Start a sentence with "I asked where babies came from; it was an innocent question."

• Or, if this will be a story you heard about rather than one you lived, try using the third-person pronoun and have it say, "she" asked or "he" asked. Just have fun with this as you remember back.

In all your archeology you just might uncover that oldest earliest self who filled those baby days with such wonderfully curious and intelligent questions. Where do we come from?

Where indeed?

All right, let's begin.

The Little Cat

I rounded the corner onto the busy main street that bisects my neighborhood and felt my heart jump at the sight: there was a cat lying in the gutter, black like my own cat and wearing the same collar, its small back facing outward toward the cars speeding past; toward the speeding cars like the car that had hit it and kept on going.

I didn't even get out of my car but drove straight home and chokingly told my husband David that I thought it was Charlotte, our own black cat whom we have loved for nearly twelve years. He calmly put aside his newspaper and walked to the kitchen window. "No, T." he said. "She's right out here napping, see?"

My knees went weak with a relief that lasted ...half a second. It didn't *matter* that the cat wasn't ours. It was *somebody's* dear pet, curled as if in sleep, toes to the curbstone.

I rushed back outside. "I'll go to Mary's" was all I could think, half running toward her house. With her big heart and her nurse's training, my neighbor Mary would know what to do.

She came to the door with her two kids - and though quick tears sprang to her eyes too, she was calm.

"I'll get something we can put it in," she said and went to do that, while her boy Ben, eleven, and her girl Rachel, nine, followed me to where the animal lay.

First Ben turned the collar of the little thing in a vain search for identification. Then Rachel crouched and stroked the fur. Then we all three crouched, a mournful silent trio.

There was a woman walking her dog across from us on this busy street. She could tell what had happened and called over, "Was it yours?"

When we said no, she told us that she had only recently moved to this neighborhood but she thought it might be her neighbor's cat so why didn't she just go see.

Mary arrived then with a big blue towel.

She spread it out and gently lifted onto it the motionless creature, perfect but for a spot of blood at the mouth.

And then we were four, keeping silent vigil.

And when, from the dog walker's side of the street, came two young women resolutely striding, one with an empty carton, I felt fresh tears rise.

When they got closer I asked, "Are you the family?" in a barely-controlled voice, dreading the witness of a sharper woe.

I can't describe to you the voice of the one who answered; the kindness that was in it; the comfort, and reassurance.

"No," she said gently, "I'm a vet though," and she straightaway knelt by the little cat and placed her fingers soft upon its breast.

"Is it dead?" the children blurted.

"Yes," she murmured. But it was not us that she spoke.

"What are you then?" she said softly to the animal, gently lifting the legs.

"Ah you're a little girl," she crooned, and with both hands raised the small and delicate head in a gesture like a caress.

"She's gone," she said, and in one easy motion lifted the cat in her blue shroud and settled her in the box, and closed the lid.

"What will you do with her?" we asked.

"Well I'll bring her to where I work and keep her for a while and then we will cremate her," she said.

And so it happened.

And in a day or two a sign went up about a lost black cat and we had the privilege of meeting the family whose pet this was, and of telling them things which to me stand as proof of all that lives and does not die. Because to them we were able to say, Not the shovel and the city truck; not the passing hours and the coating dust; but instead quick witness, and an honor guard, and escort, in the form of a young veterinarian; escort, like an angel's escort, out of this place, bright as it is, and lovely as it is, and dangerous.

> I have to say, *this* memory gets to me every time!
>
> • Now you take a minute. Press 'stop' here and just travel back to the time when you loved and lost a pet or when, like me, you witnessed someone else's loss. In loving our animals I sometime think we are at our most human. We give them our best and we never hold back or keep score.
>
> Stop your car if you're driving. Find some trees doing their usual Hula dance and just watch them for a while.
>
> Now travel back and see what comes on this theme.

Kiss Me Goodbye

I was well past weary on that short winter's day and just stepping into the hotel elevator, shifting my armfuls of stuff to push the button for my floor, when a blond lady ducked in just as the doors were closing, glanced at my burdened self and uttered a quick "What floor?"

"Four," I said gratefully, and she pushed the button.

"I'm going to Two. Hey, want a kiss?" she then turned and asked, reaching in a sack she clasped in both arms.

Who doesn't? I thought and watched as she pulled out two, wrapped in silver foil; two tiny Mt. Everests, each flying at its summit the Hershey flag of conquest. And before I had even reached my hotel room, I had peeled those babies bare and popped 'em in my mouth.

They tasted as good as real kisses to me, and they took me back to childhood, and a story my mother sometimes told about the time that her oldest child, my big sister Nan, was first treated to the world's scorn, as delivered by another little girl, crotchety and out of sorts and playing with her in her sandbox.

It was a BAD sand-box, the child told four-year-old Nan, as our mom watched helpless from the kitchen window. It was a DUMB sandbox, with DUMB scoops and shovels. In fact, all the toys at this house were DUMB, and Nan was DUMB too and she was taking her own GOOD toys and going home with them right NOW!

Now no one had ever spoken to little Nan like this in her life.

"Don't go!" she cried. But the child had stood and begun dusting off her knees. "Don't leave!' Nan pleaded.

But the girl stomped toward the back yard gate, stopping only to turn and stick out her tongue.

It was then that Nan, struggled to her own feet with a face of anguish, and called after her.

"Kiss me goodbye!" she implored, in a final hope for some kind of affirming farewell.

Poor little Nan.

But can you identify with the way that mean little girl might have felt? At the end of a bad day maybe, or even a bad year when it seems like just plain everything goes wrong? Maybe even at what feels like the end of a relationship that just doesn't seem to be working? "Good riddance to you," I know I have sometimes thought. "*Your* parting kiss I do not seek."

And then I remember that story from the Bible about Jacob's encounter with a stranger who wrestles with him the whole night through. It has always been such a puzzle to me, the way it gets toward dawn and the stranger finally says, "Let me go, for the day breaketh." And Jacob says "I will not let thee go, except thou bless me." And the angel, for that is who this is it seems, reaches down and touches his hand to the hollow of Jacob's thigh, thus somehow wounding him, but, as we are meant to understand, also blessing him, and changing him forever.

All my adult life I have been drawn to this little passage, I think because of the way it illustrates the sense of faithfulness, even in contention. It reminds me of marriage; or your relationship with your adolescent child, or your stance vis-à-vis anything that grieves or wounds you. The pain you suffer hobbles you and changes you, but in its way it blesses you too. They say there is a gift in every wound. Certainly there is a lesson.

Some days or years or relationships just limp toward their conclusion, wounded, as Jacob was intentionally wounded, enough so that he limped for the rest of his life.

"I will not go except thou bless me." Maybe that's what the bad experience is saying. Kiss me goodbye it might be asking.

Nowadays I try to do that when I feel like standing up and stalking off, denouncing the whole sandbox. In the 12-step movement they call it doing the turn-around. You make a list of all the people who have hurt you or slighted or wronged you, then slowly slowly with the help of your sponsor and the wisdom in the Big Book and the Steps themselves you come to see that there are actually ways *you* wronged or slighted or hurt them too.

We hurt each other all the time and no one more than the ones we love. We hurt ourselves. No one means to, really.

So now, if you're feeling brave, let's try doing the turn-around vis-à-vis some passage you thought to have written off as bad and slammed the door on.

* Take a peek inside now. It made such a ragged tear at the time; it just left a hole in your being. Try looking inside now and see what comes up.

Maybe you'd like the start of a sentence.

* How about, "They say what curses us blesses us but you couldn't prove it by me." Or, "There were no silver linings that I could see in the cloud that overtook me that (day, or month, or year.)

This one is going to put you in touch with some strong feelings, which isn't a bad thing.

Write what comes now. Write anything. Plus you can always tear it up. The thing is to *write it down*, and thus bring it into awareness.

Courage

As a writer, I can do my job anywhere. I can take my schedule and run it front to back or left to right. But every day if I want to stay awake, I have to move around some. So, when I get up, I dress to exercise, wearing shorts in warm weather, and adding tights when it's cooler. And for most of their childhood, this was fine with my kids.

Then they hit adolescence.

Two of our girls were in 6th grade. One was our second-born, Annie, and the other her best friend Susie, who as time went by and because she lost her mom to ALS, or Lou Gehrig's Disease, became like a real daughter to us, even sleeping in our house several times a week. One Monday morning, Annie forgot her lunch and she was skinny to begin with; so I jumped in my car, tore down to school, and as directed by the people in the Main Office, knocked on the door of their French class.

Susie spotted me first. ""Mum!" she cried with a big happy smile.

"Not the purple tights!" squeaked Annie, hiding her whole face in her French book.

That's how it is with kids and their parents: one minute they're crazy for you and the next you show up at school dressed in an unapproved manner and they're so embarrassed by you they pretend you're not related.

Of course it works the other way too.

When our oldest daughter Carrie was little, she was so demure and quiet she seemed downright fictional. About the same time my famous French class visit took place, Carrie was just turning 15. That spring she had removed the barrettes from her long hair, let it tumble over one eye, had her best friend's surgeon-dad make a tiny nose-ring-receiving hole in one nostril and bought a pet rat who was never happier than when roaming around inside her flannel shirts.

But what was I going to say to her? "*Care* about the idle speculations of strangers"? Not me. It's not how I was raised.

My mother was a single parent, left by her husband in the age of the famously intact family. She owned her own business, drove fast, and in moments of exasperation, shot cigarette smoke out of one corner of her mouth. We loved her strong hands and unusual wedding ring, a wide gold band interwoven in leaves and flowers. Once, when we were older, Mom looked down at this ring. "It's not a very conventional ring," she said cheerily, "but it wasn't a very *conventional* marriage either!" Within an hour of her sudden death, I would put it on my own hand to try and draw down her strength, which I knew I would need.

I remembered our mother often as, without her, I watched our kids move through their adolescence.

Whatever crazy things my sister and I did, she acknowledged us as belonging proudly to her, even as she acknowledged us as belonging wholly to ourselves.

So I held my tongue as my own kids expressed their natures: for the whole school year when our little boy Michael wore this bizarre novelty cap that was pierced by a large fish; or when Annie sat for her Fourth Grade school picture in a giant Scarlett-O'Hara-style bonnet.

And they in turn held theirs, as when I showed up in those purple tights. It was a Free Speech thing I guess is how we felt.

Anyway it seems to have worked, because they grew into some kind of strong and unconventional people. For her 12th birthday, Annie asked to have a pie thrown in her face; Susie developed such an intuitive bond with animals she could practically translate for them when they spoke in their deep growly voices. The two of them went off to Smith College together at age 18.

As for Nose-Ring Girl, she had paved the way by going off to Wellesley, where she tied back her hair for Rugby, majored in both Bio and Economics and planned on an MBA afterward. She used to say she wanted to manage programs that protected the Wilderness; she wanted to be sure she understood how the money flowed.

The semester before her junior year, she went out to Utah to check on this Wilderness of hers and when she came back, we saw that she had taken the delicate design of her grandmother's wedding ring and etched it in ink forever under the skin of her upper arm.

"A tattoo!" lamented her dad. You can't work in the corporate world with a tattoo!"

"Oh Dad, I'm not going to work in the corporate world" she said with the sweetest of winks. "I'm going to be the Secretary of the Interior."

So maybe I modeled a kind of behavior that first embarrassed my kids but later gave them courage. If so, they later modeled such behavior for me – and they still do, every one of them, and a good thing it is too, because God knows you need courage in life.

• So now your assignment is going to be to think of a time when *you* did the thing you feared to do; when you had to summon courage in spite of the opinions of your friends, or the disapproval perhaps of your grownups.

• Or, if it's easier for you, think of a time when somebody *else* did a daring thing that just took you aback and see if you can recall how you felt. Maybe you were a younger person at the time.

My theory of course is that we all improve the world by being ourselves and by doing that brave thing that says "Who cares what they think!"

See if that opens a vein that you might be able to mine here.

The Summer I Was Ten

Every year at September's cusp I think of it: the summer camp for girls my family owned and ran for 40 years.

When my sister Nan and I were kids, our mom and aunt ran the place, and how they agonized over it all during the off-season, mailing their hopeful brochures, driving to meet mother-daughter pairs in the tea rooms of the fine old hotels, anxiously counting and re-counting the number of campers signed up already.

(It's never been easy to get parents to give up their kids and back then it was typical to send them for a whole eight weeks!)

And then my gosh how they worried as they ran it all summer these two mothers of ours! Would they be forced to deal again with that momma bear who appeared out of nowhere, nuzzling the little kids' beach towels on the lines behind their cabins? Or with some oddball misfit of a counselor, who was secretly mean to the kids, or else cried for hours on her bed over a lost religious conviction, or else had a bad yen to slip away nights and drink with what they pictured as a set of wild and snaggle-toothed townies? Would lightning, God forbid, strike one of the buildings again, as it had that other summer?

They worried over it all.

Nan and I, we scarce gave it a thought.

Being at Camp Fernwood was a worry-free experience from our perspective and we only loved it. Both the weeks when the actual camp was in session and those beforehand, when we were the first kids of the summer to whack that new tetherball, big as the moon and buttery yellow; the first to visit the camp store pre-season, helping ourselves to bottles of Halo and White Rain shampoo, to tubes of Gleem and Ipana toothpastes, those old familiar health-and-beauty products of a long-gone era.

Then, when the season got started, we learned again how to bunt and hit a backhand; how to make a fire and do the over-arm side-stroke. There were plays and track meets, a big summer's-end banquet when even the six-year-olds won awards, and that magical last-night ceremony involving candles, when the big girls wept prettily over the pain of parting and the little ones made mischief with the dripping wax.

And then what? And then they were all gone, counselors and campers alike – vanished, every last one, by 5 that next afternoon.

Our mom and aunt sighed with relief, but for Nan and me the fun *really* started, as we took off into the empty camp, two kids alone on 100 acres with a world of sporting goods.

For hours on end we high-jumped. We played badminton. We shot long arrows – thwock! – into a by-then mighty thwock-marked target. We went to that cedar-smelling closet that was the camp store again and helped ourselves to more Halo and Gleem. We invaded the infirmary and took turns playing Broken Leg and Busted Appendix, then used the nurse's chart to measure ourselves and see if we had grown. And we knocked that old tetherball silly.

We ran to the lake and swam 'til our fingers turned blue, dove off the high board 'til the soles of our feet went raw with the scratchy bite of its surface. We were titans for those weeks, titans and amazons and gold medal winners.

And then...

And then Labor Day came and we were home again, two ordinary kids in blue school uniforms, exchanging wordless glances when, escorted by a flying wedge of veiled nuns, we passed in the no-nonsense hallways of our no-nonsense convent school.

Maybe it's the feel of who you've *been* in summer that is slowest to fade, come September.

I close my eyes and I see Nan now, graceful as a deer, arcing up and up in a swan dive, then, in just that instant, jacking her hips to reverse direction and slice narrow as a knife-blade into the water.

She is twelve, and I am ten, and for me we are twelve and ten still, somehow; just as somewhere, for us all, summer lasts and lasts, and does not end.

> • Now you go back too. Our memories of childhood summers are among the richest ones we have, perhaps because summer is such a short season and so infused with poignancy. So many things we did for the last time we did in summer; got taken to the ice cream store in our pj's for example.
>
> We sniff happy as little pups at the endless way it feels at first; and then we feel the shortening of the days as back-to-school clothes begin to appear in store windows.
>
> You won't have any trouble with this one. This piece will write itself.

If I Could've SEEN Myself!

If there's one message that's constantly singing away on every wire of our highly-wired culture it's "Look Good!"

And "Buy stuff to see that you do!" it adds as a corollary.

Obsessing over how you look has become practically a national goal here in America. It's like a contagion, and few of us are immune to it.

Certainly I haven't been.

One of my very earliest Tryin'-to-Look-Good memories goes back to the fall I was three and my big sister Nan was nearly six.

She was a beauty, even in kindergarten, tall for her age and fair as a fairytale princess.

I, by contrast, was dark and squat, with a cloud of frizz that rose from my scalp like a scouring pad over a forehead big enough to show movies on. Even now when I look at the old snapshots I think I look like a light bulb in babyshoes and a fright wig.

Anyway, this one day when six-year-old Nan modeled her new cool-weather ensemble for an admiring crowd of grownups, pirouetting in the pale-blue leggings and matching coat, I saw my chance. I went to the hall closet and dragged out her OLD coat-and-leggings set. "Here's *my* new outfit!" I blurted, lurching into the circle in my oversized garments.

I looked like a circus-monkey *dressed up as* a child rather than a child; like that light bulb in baby-shoes and a fright wig, but hey - I thought I looked great.

It's like a law of the cosmos: The more you try to dazzle 'em, the harder you fall on your face.

I think of then–President Jimmy Carter, and his big moment on first meeting the Queen Mother of England, when he trotted right over and gave her a smack on the lips in his folksy-Southern way.

"Impertinent fool!" the British press shrieked. Nobody, but nobody, it seems, gets to sashay up and smooch the Queen Mum.

Now besides meaning "rude" or "uncivil," the dictionary tells us that the word 'impertinent' also means "inappropriate," "incongruous" or "absurd."

Absurd: Like when the little kid tries to act as her own fashion designer, making wee bras for herself out of cut-up undershirts, or wearing her mom's half-slip on her head and telling people it's her hair.

Absurd: Keep the word in mind as you listen to the story's sad end.

Not long ago I planned to go to one of my bigger high school reunions, this one scheduled for late September, right at the height of the whole Lookin' Good season.

In one of the thousand catalogs wedged in our mailbox, I had seen a certain dress, black crepe with spaghetti straps and a swingy little skirt.

I had just lost 15 pounds. God knows what I was thinking: probably that I looked pretty foxy for a girl so long out of high school. Anyway, I sent away for it. And when it came, I kicked off my sneakers and jeans and pulled it over my head, without glancing again at the picture of the model wearing it in the extra catalog included in the box.

"Wow! Front-lacing!" I do remember thinking, as I tied the criss-crossed satin ribbons that spanned the deeply-plunging neckline. Unusual, to be sure, but – you know - arresting.

So I wore it to my reunion. Sadly, the eyes of the girls once so popular in high school still flickered briefly upon me and then looked away - but let me show mercy here and skip to this sad tale's end:

Just last month I donned the dress again, for the first time since that distant night.

It seemed wrong somehow: two pouches bulged in back. Turning to the front ribbons, I tried lacing my way toward decency. Then I saw it, way down by the waistband: the label, at the base of that deep wide V.

I had done it all right. A woman in her 40s, I had worn my dress backwards for an entire evening.

Doing so had been inappropriate. Absurd. Incongruous - and for one little circus monkey, deeply instructive.

• OK, now it's your turn. Remember how the sentence begins? "If I could only have SEEN myself" (that day, that night, that year.)

It shouldn't be hard. We can all remember when we felt ridiculous and suffered agonies of embarrassment.

Travel back in time now and have a visit with that early and easily mortified self. It will lose its power over you if you write it down; you know about that don't you? It's another reason we journalers journal.

OK, pen in hand. Smile while you write... "If I could have just SEEN myself...!"

An Hourglass

The month of March is a strange little month and not a beautiful one, with its puddings of mud and tangles of branches. In March we all get to wondering if winter is really ever going to end at all.

Back in 1888, the second week of March found people stopped in their tracks by a storm that draped regions from Maine to the Chesapeake Bay with such a windswept fall of snow the drifts were three times taller than the people.

Sometimes I think I dreamed this Blizzard of '88, so few people seem to know of it.

"You mean the Blizzard of *'78"* they say, speaking of a storm from the century just past.

But no, my memory goes back to the century before that one, chiefly because my mother did me the great service of reproducing at the last possible second.

She came into being in 1907 and her father some four decades earlier. As a result, he lived through that blizzard of 1888. He was a boy 13, and sometime after he grew and married and reproduced he vividly described this storm to his dark-eyed daughters Caroline and Grace. They in turn grew up and, double mothers as they were to my sister Nan and me, described it to us. Thus I see as if with my own eyes the drifts of snow piled to the secondstory windows; the week-long wait for the men and their teams of oxen to come and tramp it all down and open a roadway.

And thus seeing in imagination these snows from a storm in the 1800s, I am filled with a sweet but painful yearning for all things gone and vanished.

In March, before the real growing begins, we study those witch-fingered branches and that mudpudding earth, and think of all that has ended for us; of all that will no more be ours when the high winds of April are once again lashing with tulips.

I speak of that certain door, to a former house.

Of that certain face, more dear than words can scoop under.

Instead, in their place will be new doors and new faces.

I think now too of the Third Grade Girl Scout who one March day brought to our own door not just the cookies we had ordered in January but a note scrawled in giant block-printing for all to see.

"MAROTTA FAMILY STILL UNPAID" it said. OWES $20."

We like it so much it hangs in our kitchen, and its author's jaunty bluntness makes us smile each time we pass it.

So much is taken then, but much abides. And Nature keeps an hourglass, whose sands do spill so quickly down; but then She picks it up and turns it over.

And all it starts over again ....

This is a piece about renewal, and the mother of renewal, which we call loss.

• Try starting your entry this way: "I thought all that was over for me but I was wrong." See what happens when you say that. I bet something comes to you.

• Or, try something like this: "I thought when I left her at the station" (or, "when I quit that job" or "walked away from the grave-side"... etc.) then go on with whatever comes into your head.

Entries like this one will be numerous in your journal I hope. We tend to think the world is busy dying, but really the opposite is true. Look at nature, at societies, at your own valiant ever-renewing body and you will see: the world is busy being born.

But Not Yet

I wish I could remember in *June* that summer doesn't last.

It seems each year I convince myself it will go on forever, but alas it just doesn't. It flees us quick and soon and by September we start losing light the way a leaky bucket loses water: a minute a day at the end of August if you can believe it.

It's in late July every year when we first hear those night-time music makers the mid-summer insects, who, given the signal by some unseen conductor, tune up their little fiddles to make the sweet racket that quilts the plain cloth of darkness.

By early October, these insects will have fallen silent. By then the ivy that hugs the contours of my house will have seen its leaves pass from bright green to burgundy and dryly curl and drop away. By then the small families of field mice will have moved back indoors to make mischief in our pantry.

By late October, but no earlier. Not in September when the mice are still at summer camp outside; and when the ivy, green and shiny yet, stretches its little fingers longer with each passing day.

I look at the backs of the stacked boxes of the sound system near the window in my upstairs study each year and see that this ivy has once again magically hoisted the heavy window sash and worked its way busy way inside, reaching so far that it lattices its way up over ten or twelve CDs with its curling tendrils.

The ivy has been doing this every year for as long as we have lived in this old place, built tight enough in the 1890's but made looser by time, with many tiny portals whereby many small life forms can gain entrance.

"Cut the stuff down!" some neighbors say. "Pull that ivy clear off the house, before it wrecks your shingles!"

Ah, but we couldn't do that. We *root* for the ivy here in this house, and applaud every argument that it makes.

And what arguments are those? The argument that what wins is what keeps on growing. The argument persuading us that as long as we draw breath, we too are still in our growing season.

A few years ago my friend Ron Wiggins of the Palm Beach Post wrote something called *The First Book of Last Times,* a book that highlights the many moments when, without knowing it, we do a thing for the final time. Like getting carried indoors as sleeping children by our parents, for example.

In a later column that harked back to that theme, Ron wondered about what things his own aged parents might now be doing for the last time.

Because of a bad knee, for example, Ron said his mom has for the last time driven her beloved stick-shift pick-up. And one day, he knows, his dad will have driven his final golf ball.

But that day was not here yet as he wrote this piece. Although on many medications for dizzy spells, his dad still played golf "heavy on the gusto" as Ron puts it. "This is most apparent when Dad takes too vigorous a swing at the ball and falls over backwards, executing a neat tuck and roll."

"He's up before I can help him." "He's wiry," Ron dryly adds.

Ron says he believes his dad has a few more back somersaults in him, but he realizes too that "supplies are limited."

What isn't limited when you get right down to it though? The rose's season is brief, and even the loveliest sonnet has but 14 lines. I say we should be like the creatures described above and until we die live heavy on the gusto and grow a little every day.

• In everything I have just described you will find writing that does what many a journal entry ends up doing. It starts in one place in other words and then cartwheels to another by associations that are themselves connected step by step in the writer's mind, in much the same was as the Hourglass piece immediately preceding this did.

• Try writing a piece that begins with some seasonal observation like the business here with summer's little musicians and the ivy on my house. Before any of us are citizens or consumers or even companions one to another, remember that we are animals first, and tightly bound to nature. You yourself mark every tiny tick of every season; you're hard-wired to. You could tell I bet within five days whether this was, say, a late March day or an early April day.

Here's a chance to name some of the clues that tell you where you are in the great cycle of the year with its swirling stars and ever-changing seasons.

The Stream of
Our Common Life

I could never live a life withdrawn from the world like some have done. The solitary Henry Thoreau did it for a year, living in his tiny cabin on the banks of Walden Pond in Concord, Massachusetts.

Thoreau was famously withdrawn - famously separate. He once said that he never found the companion as companionable to him as solitude. All the talk and interaction in the town made him feel trapped and flustered I think. It's just like that for some people.

Well it's not like that for me.

If I lived apart as some choose to, I would be sad all the time, and feel like the small child sent to bed early while the party roared on downstairs.

No, I prefer to go out and see people, mix it up, dip my toe in the stream of our common life.

One spring day I stood on a subway car and watched a man a foot away from me as he filled in a crossword puzzle so speedily it stunned me. Of course it was a typical subway ride: nobody spoke and nobody looked at anyone else - until suddenly he looked at me and said, "I like that satin stripe down the side of your pants!" (They were some nice old tuxedo pants I found in a thrift store somewhere.)

"You missed 49 Across," I said back to him. "And I think I know what it is."

Later, noting my suitcase, he asked where I was going. I told him Newark, to see a prospect and show my writing wares, like any salesman.

"You're brave, going to Newark!" he said as if going there from Boston was like trying to make Calcutta by lunch.

There was no brave about it of course. I just sat on a train for five hours and witnessed many more wonders:

For example:

I saw one family's socks, undies and T-shirts dancing on a clothesline in a warm spring rain. I saw a sponge mop hanging on a nail outside a bathroom window, an excellent solution to an age-old storage problem. I saw a gaggle of railroad workers standing around joking and in their bright yellow slickers they looked to me like so many First Graders waiting for the School Bus.

Inside my train car, a little boy about three sat listening to his dad, who spoke to him earnestly, teachingly, in the soft syllables of what sounded like Vietnamese. Suddenly, in the middle of the third or fourth paragraph of the dad's lesson, the child stretched up and kissed him - smack! - on his busy talking teeth.

There is much kissing in the world, you notice, if you look around even a little.

In one seat toward the back of the train, a man about 30 kept sighing happily and interrupting his girlfriend at her reading to engage her in prolonged kissing sessions. You knew at a glance that they were calm and happy and very nearly exempt from Time altogether.

But the day after my journey to Newark, in a car at the edge of a parking lot, I remember seeing two other people kissing and what I saw struck me so I have never forgot it:

The man climbed out of his own vehicle to get into the woman's. They kissed, then stopped to talk earnestly, then kissed some more, all in that frantic way that made you know that kissing was not enough. You knew too that they were not calm and happy, but agitated and miserable; that they were very much on the clock; *and* that they did not belong with each other.

You learn lessons for your own life, walking around in the busy world.

This next exercise will be fun because you have some good choices.

• One choice is to try watching strangers to discern their relationship to each other. The other is to just collect them all up in a mental bouquet (scratching down notes if you can) to see what variety of mood and feeling there is in any group of people. Because of course people wear their inner states on their faces and in the way they carry themselves. We can read them almost effortlessly – our instincts do this for us. What you want to do is describe just the set of mouth or cast of eyes that betrays these feelings.

This exercise will be even easier if you are in one of the big anonymous public spaces where people are already looking at each other in that bored way.

Your challenge will be to look bored too, though really you will be fascinated. When I taught a small group of fifth graders a little unit on writing once I brought them on a train ride into the city. I told them they should wear sunglasses like I do so I can watch people without them knowing that I'm watching them.

They brought the sunglasses, bless their little hearts. Lined up on the train seats they looked like a double combo of the Three Blind Mice.

And boy did they notice things and people!

Your goal is to be like them in this exercise though it won't be easy. Not too many people see as clearly as a bunch of 11-year-olds, but give it a try!

Auld Lang Syne

You live long enough you can't help but notice how much holidays change over time. Gradually, to be sure. Subtly, at first. But undeniably.

Take tree trimming, for example. People once put their trees up just days, even just hours, before Christmas itself. When I was little, our tree didn't go up until we were in bed on the 24th - the idea being that Santa brought it along with everything else, the miracle you padded downstairs in footed pjs to see, lit and glowing softly in the darkened parlor.

And then, it stayed up until January 6th - Little Christmas - when the Wise Men, those victims of lousy directions, showed up at last at the stable door in Bethlehem. Once, everyone kept their trees up that long - 'til all twelve days of Christmas had been duly ticked off and accounted for.

That never happens now. Now by New Years Day, often most trees have been unceremoniously stripped of their medals and given the bum's rush out the door. Why? Because they were set up back in November, when the bony crags of turkey carcass still roosted grandly in the fridge.

Everything is different now, everything subtly changed from what it once was.

Cast your eyes back to long ago holidays and what do you see? Ribbon candy, unheard of now.

Fruitcake, which in the short space of a decade, has inexplicably gone from a respected and much praised delicacy to an object of general derision. Plum pudding. Staying up with sweet old Guy Lombardo for the ball to drop and the New Year to commence. All replaced now, all gone: The angel hair and the big hot lights. The ornaments so thin they popped like soap bubbles. The crinkly kind of tinsel that hurt your fillings if it got in your mouth.

Back when I was in my early 20s, my young husband David and I drove over to my cousin Sheila's house on New Year's Eve, to see the New Year in with lots of our siblings and cousins. We were young and zany then. We stayed up most of the night, yelping our way through songs, playing charades, and offering cheese balls to the blinking puppy my sister Nan had received days before from her new husband Tom. At midnight, I remember, Tom got the guys to carry him into the living room, dressed only in a diaper and a baby bonnet, "Happy New Year" crookedly scrawled on his chest in bright pink lipstick.

How bright and carefree we were then!

We're for sure not as carefree now, because now suddenly *we* are the grownups and the stress of the holidays falls squarely on our shoulders.

For example, each year we trim the tree on a Sunday and on Monday morning come downstairs to find it lying sprawled on the floor. We stand it back up, its lights dangling, its ornaments askew. Sometimes even on the Tuesday morning it's back there again, face down on the rug like a drunk. We buy stand after stand every year but it never seems to matter. We ended up solving the problem by getting each tree to dangle more than stand – suspending it by its ears, so to speak – lashing it with lengths of wire to the two window frames it stands between.

Things change, then, with the holidays as with everything else. That blinking puppy of so long ago grew up and died old. Tom, our New Year's Baby of our silly pageant, died young, on a tennis court, one sunny summer morning and how we miss him still, as we miss all that passes too soon from our lives. But here always come new traditions, and new faces - and that cup of kindness, which we all should take, for Auld Lang Syne.

> • Well now, this subject is sure to provide fertile topics for journaling! I don't think you even need much of a beginning from me to get you going.

> • Try focusing it on the holiday that is most meaningful for you and start maybe by saying something like, "I thought they'd last forever, those holidays with ...." Describe the food. The way the house smelled. You in your little pjs. Where you hid and peeked from, when, as a small child, you watched the preparations go forth.

Don't doubt that you *can* call all this up; it is all still in there. And then you can honor its memory by mentioning those absent faces as I have done with that tribute to Tom, that New Year's Baby of our silly pageant, which took me only half a sentence but allowed me to feel the whole memory so much more fully.

Never be afraid to really feel your feelings. We're beginning to all understand now that feelings that don't get acknowledged tend to rattle around under the floorboards, making mischief for both mind and body.

Remember that wonderful bit of wisdom that says that the only way out is through. If you can really mark and mourn your losses you can live out every day that follows free and glad and present to that day's beauty. OK then.

How about "Every year it seems the holiday unfolded the same way...."

• Try that for a beginning, and be prepared for some strong feelings to arise. It should come as no surprise to realize that some of our most poignant feelings are gathered around the memory of childhood celebrations.

Your Sibling Your Self

I threw myself a party for my 50th birthday and the whole night all I could think of was how lucky I felt that almost everyone I loved on this earth had come.

Even my sister Nan came, from faraway Florida, Nan, who added a lively dash of adrenaline to those snoozy years of childhood when she was tall and Tinker-Toy-thin and I was small and round, with dark curls so densely tangled our grandfather called me Blackberry Top.

The night before she flew into town, Nan sent me an email. And because what she wrote is so vivid, I thought I would record it here, in case any of you would enjoy hearing a voice like my voice, but distinctly different too; in case any of you have felt the way a reader in Michigan seems to have felt when she sent me an email that said, "Keep those memory pieces coming - especially the ones about you and your sister Nan!"

So here's what Nan wrote, on the day before her baby sister joined the ranks of the truly middle-aged:

"Okay, Woman, this is your card," it begins.

"You know I can't stand and deliver in front of people the way you can, but I've been thinking and thinking of how to say what's in my heart here.

"I recall once asking Mom about my earliest 'real' memory, which is of her in a pink robe seated in that chaise longue in her old bedroom. She told me that was the day she came home from the hospital with you." (I should maybe say that Nan had just turned two when I was born so this IS an early memory.)

And now we're back to her birthday letter to me:

"Of course we both remember all the weird times: me rolling you down the staircase inside that big comforter, me chasing you around with the hypodermic needles from Auntie's medical bag, me dangling you out the window, etc. "Course all you had to was yell, 'Mom!' and I was doing hard time in my room for the rest of the afternoon."

I'll stop here and say Nan HAD tortured me some, especially on days when Mom worked my fat baby arms into this little pink cardigan, which Nan called my "pinch sweater" because pinching me when I wore it was as irresistible as tickling the Pillsbury Dough Boy.

"Remember our charts?" she went on this email. "How you got little stars on yours for not wetting your bed and I got stars on mine for not waking you up mornings?

"Remember the teen-age years, and our shared closet? You'd leave for school before me and I'd borrow your clothes. Of course, you'd sprinkled baby powder on your side of the floor so you could detect my footprints; and when I'd caught on to THAT little scheme, you began buttoning your blouses on one, three, five and seven, knowing I'd mess that up too.

"I remember how Mom would always tell us that that the closest bond is that of siblings - not parent and child, not husband and wife, but the common chromosomal makeup of sibs. I think this was a message to us without a father, from Mom who loved us so much; her way of saying that no matter what, we'd have each other.

"I have an intense and enormously special memory that is always with me," she went on. "To this day and frequently I see the two of us in summer. We're little and sitting on the warm cement slab at the bottom of the porch steps, drinking orange juice that Mom has just squeezed. The sun is on our right and we're planning our day and smelling the wonderful lilac and honeysuckle. You're even wearing the Pinch Sweater in this memory but I let you live – for that one day anyway.

"Happy birthday, Blackberry Top. I love you, dearest sister," is how she ended this note which I read to you here to help get us into this very special exercise.

Now I want you to try something a little different.

• Be like this sister of mine and write a fond letter like this to one of your siblings. It doesn't matter if you and this sibling are no longer close; it doesn't even matter if this sibling is no longer in the world. In fact all the more reason to write this pretend letter if either of these two situations apply.

• Begin with actual letter form and use the phrases "I remember" like Nan did, or "do you recall" or "I can still see the two of us..."

• Don't force it or feel it has to be a series of perfect paragraphs. Just scribble if that's what it takes. The memories may very well come thick and fast and you will *need* to scribble to keep up. Remember that your journal need not be neat; should not be neat. If it's messy it just shows how much you have loved it and returned to it and worked with it.

I have talked a lot about my sister Nan in this audio book and Nan stories are scattered through all my columns and my regular "reading" books too.

She was my first, best friend, and the explainer and interpreter of my world.

Maybe your sibling was that for you or you were that for your sibling.

Anyway, no one else knows what your childhood kitchen looked like just at 5pm say, when you sat on your two chairs, little legs dangling down, not yet reaching the floor. No one else remembers how your mother's hips moved as she rolled out pie dough. (She certainly wouldn't know. How would she know how she looked from the back?)

You saw the world from the back and way down low with eyes filled with that old early wonder...that old early trust. And this brother or this sister that you address was right there beside you.

• Talk to that person now; write him or her a letter perhaps. It may carry under every word a declaration of love like my sister Nan's letter does, because what is love but attention paid? And what did we ever want in life but to be seen? Recognized? "You don't even have to *like* me all that much, but just *know* me" is how most of us feel, just as we all know the ones who are special in our lives, whom we could pick out in a crowd of a thousand, at night, from the back.

This little letter may carry other things too. Let it carry what it carries; that's not your business to fret over or puzzle out. Your business is to say what is true for you. And even if some of those things you remember are painful still this journal of yours will read like a love letter, both to you later when you look back at it and certainly to the ones who cherished you in your time here.

This brings us to the end then of *Still Following the Trail of Breadcrumbs to Journal Your Way Back Home.*

I wish I could be there to see what you write, but maybe I'm not apart from you really if Abraham Lincoln spoke the truth when he said that writing conquers all distances of time and space.

I'm in a tiny cabin in New Hampshire recording this, can you see me?

I can almost see you I think. You seem to be smiling almost and now you're looking around for something to write with. Write then. It is a holy act.

About the Author

For more than a quarter of a century Terry Marotta has been producing a column that today appears in papers all over the country.

Her preparation for this great life began in the heart of Boston, then moved 20 miles north to the Lowell public schools and later still 100 miles west to wonderful Smith College, from which she graduated in the great headband and bell-bottom era.

She then spent the better part of her 20s teaching English at a big public high school, where she found herself so changed by her contact with the dreams and hopes of the teens she met there that she soon realized she wanted to work with young people always. Accordingly, she is still surrogate mother to four alumni scholars from the National Program for a Better Chance, the assistant Youth Group leader in her church and a person who is happy to help anybody, anybody at all who is struggling to write a decent paper.

In 1986, at the height of NASA's glory days Terry was chosen as a Finalist in the Journalist-in-Space contest, one of only two in New England so honored. Although the tragic loss of *Challenger* caused that initiative to be stalled, she still considers herself to be in training for the job. Her helmet is packed.

Besides producing the column and this most recent book on journaling, Terry does regular commentaries for Public Radio, and she has written pieces for *Chicken Soup* for the Mother's Soul, the big women's magazines, the Boston Globe and the Christian Science Monitor. Additionally, she has penned three other books: two collections of reader-favorite essays called *Vacationing in My Driveway* and *I Thought He Was a Speed Bump*; and *The Mountains I Raise*, this last an anthology of short pieces by ten very sage individuals whose company she enjoyed while teaching them for three years at the local Senior Center. Finally she has had the honor of functioning both as one of the Girls Scouts' Leading Women and one of Smith College's Alumnae in Residence, in both cases greatly enjoying the time spent with people almost the same age as those long-ago students who first taught her what it meant to have a calling in life.

In general Terry believes in the transformative powers of unconditional love, in eavesdropping with the intention of catching people at their best, and in tapping into the great font of collective wisdom that resides in the common people. She lives eight miles north of Boston with her family and, like millions of other weary grownups, waits all day to relax with a good book or movie, then falls asleep the minute she sits down in her chair.

Additional Works

Terry Marotta has been talking to the American newspaper public since 1980; in the column that she syndicates nationwide, in her three books, and most recently by means of this journaling "workshop in a box" that teaches people how easy it is for anyone to write the kind of first-person essay that stops time and acts as a kind of fixative for experience.

Her first reader-favorite collection, *I Thought He Was a Speed Bump and Other Excuses from Life in the Fast Lane,* contains accounts of family life with young children and is mostly a series of madcap dogs-getting-pantyhose-stuck-on-their-muzzles-type pieces, some wry ones on the tug-of-war that is marriage, and a handful of pretty serious ones about the one or two truths she says she has come to grasp along the way. With chapter headings such as "Thy Kingdom Come I Will be Dumb," "When Will Dad Become a Woman?" and "Shall We Gather by the River?" this book has proved popular with a wide range of readers, from the Fourth Grade to the Assisted Living Facility.

A few years further on with *"The Mountains I Raise,"* Terry gathered the personal reminiscences of ten senior citizens whom she taught in a course called "Writing from Personal Experience." In the poem that gives this book its name, Robert Frost meditates on the difficulty of raking up a yard full of leaves. Like the gathering up of a lifetime of experiences, he finds it no small task. "Next to nothing for use/ and since they grow duller/ from contact with earth/ next to nothing for color" he says the leaves are; and many of the eleven contributors to this book began by thinking their own experiences were "next to nothing" in terms of meaning, until slowly, over time, their willingness to tell their stories made them know otherwise.

Thirdly, *Vacationing in My Driveway* offers 52 funny, poignant, true-life tales, one for each week of the year. Its title comes from that moment when, exhausted after the day's efforts, you pull up in your driveway, turn off the car and think, "Maybe I'll just *sit* here a minute. Maybe I don't *have* to dash right inside and start banging the pots around to make dinner. And it is in the peace of that sitting-still moment that you realize: you can't set out to find the joyous vacation-like moments in life. Instead, you must let these times find you, as they surely will, catching you as likely in the busy press of obligation as in the easy peace of leisure.

As the reader moves through the book, he or she sees that the winter-month stories treat winter tribulations and winter rewards, while the spring ones are filled with moments of longing. Summer's chapters have funny and tender moments as the reins are relaxed, and autumn's brim with that great Back-to-School feeling that things are just plain *starting over...*

Not everything starts over, of course. All that blossoms must fade, and this book reflects that truth too. But even as there are some few stories of loss and mourning, there are many more that tell of renewal and invite the reader to believe what Terry so firmly believes: that whatever death takes from us now will, in some form, be given back.

The Palm Beach Post once said that that Terry might just be the best unfamous writer in America. Whether or not that's true, she does believe she just might be the one having the most fun on the journey.

Ordering Additional Copies

We all know it: the best reward for telling a part of your story is hearing someone else tell a part of his. Hence, in each of the book's 27 chapters, listeners first hear Terry tell some tales of her own before coming to the actual writing prompts that will get them recording their own thoughts and observations.

When we write down how we feel we suddenly see our life more clearly. Better yet, we then feel grateful for it, and lucky that we were put here at all.

And then? Then we grow willing to speak our truth, either to the people in the checkout line or the ones living right under our roof. We help make community, in other words. We send up some lovely messages to the Creator. And then we grow suddenly and unaccountably cheerful.

Order the book for someone you love and start spreading the cheer!

Available from your favorite bookstore – and our secure server at TheTrailofBreadcrumbs.com

Order Form

Please send me:

_______ copies of ***Still Following the Trail of Breadcrumbs to Journal Your Way Back Home*** *(Book with 2 CDs)*
$29.95 each (plus 5% tax in MA), plus $5.00 shipping/handling per book.

_______ copies of ***Vacationing in My Driveway*** *(Book)*
$12.95 each (plus 5% tax in MA), plus $3.00 shipping/handling per book.

_______ copies of ***I Thought He Was a Speed Bump*** *(Book)*
$9.95 each (plus 5% tax in MA), plus $3.00 shipping/handling per book.

_______ copies of ***The Mountains I Raise*** *(Book)*
$9.00 each (plus 5% tax in MA), plus $3.00 shipping/handling per book.

Name: _________________________________ Phone: _________

Address: ____

City: _________________State: ________ Zip: _________

E-Mail Address: _______________________________________

Checks Accepted • Ravenscroft Press 617-512-2264

Mail Your Order and Payment to:

Ravenscroft Press
P.O. Box 270, Winchester, MA 01890

SECURE SHOPPING CART
MORE BOOKS BY TERRY MAROTTA VISIT:
TheTrailofBreadcrumbs.com
TerryMarotta.com